DIGITAL PROCUREMENT UNLOCKED

TRANSFORMING BUSINESS WITH PROCUREMENT DATA

DEEPTI BANDI

Made with ♥ on the Notion Press Platform
www.notionpress.com

To my beloved mother **Smt C. Kasturi Lokababu**, whose unwavering love, support, and strength have been a constant source of inspiration. This book, "**Digital Procurement Unlocked**" is a heartfelt dedication to you. Your endless love and sacrifices have paved the way for this journey, and I am forever grateful.

Contents

Contents

Preface

Welcome to a comprehensive guide on the end-to-end digitalization of Procurement. This book is designed to cater to a diverse audience, encompassing both procurement professionals seeking to leverage data and technology and digital experts unfamiliar with the intricacies of procurement.

For procurement professionals, who are well-versed in procurement practices but seek insights into harnessing data and technology, this book offers valuable strategies and practical applications. Similarly, digital professionals, including data analysts and data scientists, will find an in-depth understanding of the entire procurement process to augment their expertise.

Drawing from my committed research and extensive experience across various domains, this book unravels the potential of digitalization, empowering readers to revolutionize their procurement practices and drive sustainable competitive advantage.

Acknowledgements

Writing this book has been a remarkable journey, and I am deeply grateful to all those who have supported and encouraged me along the way.

First and foremost, I extend my heartfelt gratitude to my mentors and colleagues whose guidance and wisdom have been invaluable. Their unwavering support and belief in my abilities have inspired me to pursue this endeavor with passion and dedication.

I would also like to express my gratitude to my dear friends who generously offered their time and expertise to proofread the book. Your invaluable feedback and constructive criticism have played a crucial role in refining the content and making this book a better piece of work.

A special word of thanks goes to my children for their exceptional maturity and patience throughout this writing journey. Your understanding and unwavering support have been my constant motivation, even during the extra time I invested in this book.

Last but not least, I am indebted to countless authors whose books have shaped me into the person I am today. The wisdom, knowledge, and inspiration I gained from their works have been instrumental in shaping the ideas and concepts explored in this book.

To all of you, I extend my heartfelt appreciation for being an integral part of this literary venture. Your support and encouragement have been the driving force behind this book's creation, and I am forever grateful for your contributions.

Thank you all for being an essential part of this journey.

"Digital transformation is more about the journey than the destination. It is a continuous quest for innovation, adaptation, and redefining the boundaries of what is possible."

- Satya Nadella, CEO of Microsoft

Let's Begin the Journey

CHAPTER I

A Quest for Excellence

When I started my career in data science, it was a world of POCs. We had neither relevant data nor a business use case that would impact the organizational goals. It was all technology-driven, and building fancy models is what created a buzz. However, as I progressed in my career and joined as a digital procurement professional, it became apparent to me that technology alone doesn't have the sole influence. I began questioning myself: What do I need to do with my technical skills? How are my data science skills different from software skills in terms of influencing digitalization? This is where I realized that a proper combination of data, business, and technology is what makes the influence obvious.

You must have definitely encountered many individuals discussing the vast amount of data available within their organizations. However, the question remains: Are we utilizing this data effectively to create an impact? The obvious answer that comes to mind is probably not! So, I started to delve deeper to understand where we need to exert influence to drive progress. Is it improving the data collection process, aligning with the business goals, or implementing the right technology that influences the success of digital procurement? The collection of data attributes is an ongoing endeavour, but the more attributes we accumulate, the greater the confusion regarding what we can actually do with these scattered fragments of data within an organization.

First and foremost, without setting a goal, how can anyone determine whether this data is sufficient or insufficient? Let's assume we have somehow determined the necessary data attributes. Now the question arises: How can I ensure that the data collected is accurate and obtained in the appropriate manner? What are the right sources to store the data? If these considerations are not addressed beforehand, there is no point in collecting data and storing it in a location where it cannot be effectively utilized. Therefore, from this, we understand that without a clear vision in place, amassing large volumes of data serves no purpose.

Let's assume that we have a clear goal set regarding the data. However, what if the data is incomplete or captured incorrectly due to various reasons? What if we are gathering data from obsolete legacy systems? These questions lead us to the realization that the data we collect needs to undergo a defined refinement process before it can be effectively utilized. This realization itself becomes a vision for any large organization. So, how do we go about achieving this? In Part 1 of this book, titled "Handling Procurement Data," we will delve into the intricacies of managing data in a strategic manner. We will explore concepts such as data lakes and their role in facilitating data-driven decision-making. This will provide us with a solid foundation to harness the power of data in our digital procurement journey.

During a conversation with my senior colleague, I learned that the true success of digital transformation lies in achieving a minimum 10x impact on the organization's growth. This sparked my thinking process: Are we anywhere close to achieving this? The obvious answer is NO. We often create visually appealing dashboards that provide little or no actionable insights. We invest in highly advanced technologies like AI models to solve problems that may have minimal or no significance to the company as a whole.

Deriving actionable insights should be a goal, whether it's from a simple dashboard or an AI model. If we are unable to take action based on what we see, all our efforts will go to waste. And to achieve a 10x impact, we must align this with our business goals. In procurement, our ultimate objective is to maximize savings. This is what drives our business. Savings can take various forms, such as monetary savings, time savings, resource optimization, and more. As procurement professionals, we are aware that achieving savings for the company is not as straightforward as it may seem. Why is that? The answer is simple: savings come from multiple dimensions, including suppliers, resources, negotiations, and quick turnarounds, to name a few. This presents us with a multi-dimensional problem that needs to be solved. And to solve such a problem, the solution must go beyond having the right data in place. We need analytics, from descriptive to prescriptive, to truly leverage our data. This is where the data starts being effectively utilized. A strategic approach is required to make our analytics speak to us.

Consider this: How many items in your dashboards actually aid you in day-to-day decision making? Less than 20%? You're not alone in this struggle. Most organizations face challenges in making their data speak to them in a meaningful way. Therefore, in Part 2 of this book, titled "Analytic Adventure," I will delve into the strategic consumption of the data we collect, which involves significant investments. This section discusses leveraging analytics in procurement. We will explore methodologies, tools, and techniques that enable us to derive valuable insights from the vast amount of data at our disposal. We will delve into the art of data visualization and diagnostic analytics, empowering us to make informed decisions, identify trends, optimize supplier relationships, and achieve strategic objectives.

Another crucial factor that drives the success of digital transformation in any organization is innovation. Without innovation, we would merely be using the existing wheel without creating beautiful cars that can take us forward. However, we all know that innovation doesn't happen spontaneously. We need to cultivate ideas and foster a culture of innovation within the organization. It's important to note that innovation, if not aligned with business goals, can be a waste of time and resources.

As described by Anthony. W. Ulwick in his book – "Jobs to be Done: Theory to Practice", innovation should be outcome-driven. The outcomes should directly impact the business goals of the organization. So, where does innovation fit in the procurement world? It certainly has a place, but it requires a significant amount of out-of-the-box thinking. Procurement deals with data coming from various sources, including transactional data, master data, contract data, and so on. Therefore, we need to approach innovation in a strategic manner while encouraging unconventional thinking.

While we cannot define a strict process for innovation, let's explore how we can approach it strategically.

Allow me to illustrate this with an example. Imagine we are given puzzle pieces and asked to assemble them based on a picture. It may take some time, but eventually, we can solve the puzzle. This represents sustainable innovation. Similarly, within procurement, we can start building basic descriptive analytics using one type of data available, such as spend, sourcing, or contracts. This helps us gain better insights.

Now, let's consider a scenario where we have puzzle pieces from two different boxes, both depicting the Avengers, but we don't have a single picture to guide us. The challenge here is to use pieces from both boxes and assemble them to create one meaningful picture. This is akin to dealing with different data sources simultaneously in procurement. This is where the concept of efficiency innovation comes into play. By combining data from various sources within procurement, we aim to derive actionable insights. However, the challenge lies in understanding the future solution we are trying to build since the data comes from different sources, each with its own subject matter experts (SMEs).

Let's take another step forward in our analogy. Imagine you have puzzle pieces from different themes, such as Barbie, Avengers, and a landscape. This time, you need to put all the puzzle pieces together to create a complete and meaningful story. This represents outcome-driven innovation, which can result in not just a 10x impact but even a 100x impact in some cases if successfully achieved. In the digital transformation journey, reaching this level of innovation is essential to make a significant business impact. It goes beyond just utilizing procurement data; it involves leveraging rich organizational data from other departments, such as finance, risk assessments, and supply chain.

In Part 3 of the book, titled "AI Innovation," I aim to explain the various AI technologies available to support the innovation process. I will delve deeper into different use cases that are relevant to procurement. It's important to note that these use cases may differ for each organization, as they are specific to their unique needs. The intention here is not to provide a step-by-step guide but rather to provoke thoughts and suggest a direction. This section uncovers the fascinating world of AI innovation in procurement. We will explore the integration of artificial intelligence, machine learning, and robotic process automation, which revolutionize procurement processes, making them efficient, intelligent, and autonomous. Through real-world use cases, we will understand the potential of AI-driven chatbots, automated supplier evaluations, and smart contract management, immersing ourselves in the cutting-edge technologies that shape the future of digital procurement. In the end we also have a section that aims to provide insights into ensuring that the transformation aligns with ethical principles.

As we proceed to the next parts of the book, let's take a moment to gain an understanding of the challenges we may encounter in this journey of digital procurement. It is crucial for us to anticipate these challenges so that we are aware and, in most cases, well-prepared to overcome them. When we embark on the implementation phase, it will not be merely another project or product development; it will entail a complete shift in the procurement process—a digital transformation in procurement. Therefore, it is worthwhile to invest some thought into the challenges we may face along the way.

Apart from the technical glitches that we will discuss in the later parts of this book, one of the most common challenges I have encountered is resistance to change. As humans, we are adaptable creatures, yet paradoxically, we often find it difficult to embrace even minor changes in our day-to-day work. Meanwhile, technological advancements continue to progress rapidly. So, how do we overcome this resistance among our procurement associates?

Some individuals may resist change due to a fear of losing their jobs to sophisticated technology, while others may prefer to stick with familiar routines rather than investing time in updating their skills with new tools. From their perspective, these concerns are valid. However, as initiators of the digital transformation process, it is our responsibility to encourage procurement professionals to embrace technology. The question then arises: How do we accomplish this?

Based on my observations within my organization, I strongly believe that forcing someone into a new process does not yield favorable results for either side. Instead, it is important to empathize and put ourselves in their shoes. Sympathy plays a crucial role in the overall transformation process. Rather than building entirely new tools with cutting-edge technology just because we can, it would be more effective to integrate our tools into the existing processes.

Let me provide an example. When Swiggy, a food delivery app in India, introduced its InstaMart store for grocery delivery, they did not create a new app. Introducing a new app would have required customers to register again, potentially leading to a loss of existing customers. Instead, Swiggy integrated its InstaMart store within the existing food delivery app. This made it easier for customers to adapt to the enhancement without the need for a completely new tool. I believe this approach is ideal for the digital transformation of procurement, as well as for any domain. It is crucial for us to understand the existing processes and tools that procurement professionals use on a daily basis, and then enhance them with the power of data, analytics, and AI innovation. Creating numerous different portals or tools would make the adaptation process more challenging.

However, I also acknowledge that not all aspects of the transformation process can be incorporated into existing portals or tools. In such cases, the leadership team plays a significant role. When the new transformation tools come from the highest levels of leadership, it facilitates smoother synchronization and reduces resistance to change. Therefore, it is crucial to eliminate resistance to change from the top-down, ensuring alignment from the leadership level to the grassroots level, rather than the other way around.

Collaboration with other departments in the organization is yet another challenge we face on this journey of transformation. Imagine if the procurement department started the transformation journey independently, without any knowledge of what the other departments are doing. In this case, it would be challenging for procurement to integrate their data with other relevant data to derive meaningful insights for the organization as a whole. We need to work on breaking down the silos and fostering collaboration among different departments in the organization.

As the famous quote from Albert Einstein goes, "In the middle of every difficulty lies opportunity." Each challenge presents an opportunity for growth and innovation. It invites us to think creatively, seek out best practices, and forge new paths forward. Don't you agree that conquering these challenges is not only essential but also rewarding? Breaking through resistance to change will result in a proactive and agile procurement function, ready to adapt to evolving business landscapes. Fostering collaboration will cultivate a culture of shared success, where all stakeholders work hand in hand to achieve common goals.

With these questions, thoughts, and ideas, let us embark together on the intricate landscape of digital procurement, equipping ourselves with the knowledge, insights, and tools to navigate this transformative path. Are you ready to discover the untapped potential that awaits us?

Handling Procurement Data

PART-1

"In God we trust, all others must bring data."

- W. Edwards Deming

CHAPTER II

Introduction to Procurement Data Management

Data in procurement might not be as large as big data coming from IoT, but it is a humongous amount where a strategic process is needed to deal with it. As a procurement professional, even if you are managing only one cluster in a category, you must have come across data flowing from different systems. We need to make this siloed data talk to each other so that we can create an impact using this data. Integrating this data from different systems is what makes different systems speak to each other. A bigger impact is created when you **integrate data**. What's the big impact? Well, the list may be exhaustive, but here are few benefits of integrating data:

- Enhance supplier evaluation: integrating data from different sources allows for a comprehensive evaluation of suppliers' performance, reliability, and financial stability, enabling informed decision-making.
- Cost Optimization: Integrating data helps identify cost-saving opportunities by comparing prices, negotiating better terms, and analyzing historical purchasing data.
- Risk Mitigation: Integrating data from various sources enables the identification of potential risks related to suppliers, such as quality issues, delivery delays, or geopolitical factors, facilitating proactive risk mitigation strategies.

- Performance Measurement: Integrating data allows for comprehensive performance measurement, tracking key procurement metrics such as on-time delivery, cost savings, supplier performance, and overall process efficiency, facilitating continuous improvement efforts.

So, as we move on in the digital procurement journey, we now realize that data integration is one of the most crucial challenges we are facing. Without integrating data from various sources, it would be impossible to gain a comprehensive understanding of the procurement process and identify areas for improvement.

Well, nothing comes as easy as told. There could be several challenges that you are facing as we deal with these numbers. How we attack these challenges is what we are going to discuss in this part of the book. The next chapter talks about the various challenges that we face with procurement data available around us. Different scenarios are taken up, and the corresponding challenges are explained. We will not see how to solve these problems here. We will touch upon that in the subsequent chapters.

But before we understand how to face our challenges with data, let us also spend some time understanding all the different sources of procurement data. In Chapter 4, I will walk you through the various kinds of data that are available not only within procurement but also through various external sources. Well, this chapter might be very obvious for professionals who have spent a good amount of time in procurement. But the intention here is to cover this briefly so that folks with only a digitalization background would understand the way procurement data is procured.

Also, data integration is not just about bringing different datasets together but also about ensuring that the data is accurate, consistent, and relevant. You must have already pictured how complex of a task this is, given that data comes from different sources, in different formats, and with different levels of quality. Let's talk about how we could map this data from various sources in Chapter 5.

One of the most significant benefits of data integration in procurement is the ability to gain a real-time, comprehensive view of the procurement process. By integrating data from different sources such as suppliers, invoices, SOWs, contracts, and inventory, procurement professionals can get a complete picture of the entire procurement lifecycle. This helps us identify bottlenecks, inefficiencies, and areas for improvement and take corrective action promptly. But do you think integrating the data manually is worth the effort? What can we do to better integrate our data? Let's dive into the concept of a Data Lake in Chapter 6 to understand how and what can be done better. How will a data lake help us access real-time analytics and insights into supplier performance, purchasing patterns, and spend management savings?

Despite its many benefits, data integration is not without its challenges. It requires significant effort and investment, both in terms of technology and resources, money, and time. Organizations need to invest in the right tools and technologies to integrate data from different sources effectively. Additionally, they need to ensure that they have the right people with the necessary skills and expertise to manage and maintain the data integration process. Moreover, data integration also raises concerns about data privacy, security, and governance. We need to ensure that we comply with data protection regulations and use data ethically and responsibly. We also need to have robust data governance policies and procedures in place to ensure that data is accurate, consistent, and secure.

So, in this part of the book, I will discuss the key challenges of data integration in procurement, including the various sources of procurement data and mapping files, and the process of building a data lake. We will discuss how to integrate different sources of procurement data and highlight the benefits of building a data lake. Let's not forget the role of data governance in ensuring the quality and accuracy of procurement data and how to implement data governance processes in your organization. By the end of Part 1, readers will have a better understanding of the importance of data integration in procurement, as well as practical advice on how to overcome the challenges associated with it.

Fasten up to dive into the next chapter to see what challenges the integration of Procurement Data poses!

CHAPTER III

The Data Challenges

In the previous chapter we have seen that integrating data from various sources is the solution to deal with data from siloed systems. But integrating data from so many different sources coming in various formats is not going to be a cake walk. There will certainly be some hurdles, and its good to know what we are going to face beforehand. In order to overcome these, we need to have a strategy for having unified data. In this chapter, let us discuss the key data challenges that we encounter while we explore strategies to effectively integrate the data.

Data on multiple systems

Did you ever face challenges in matching and comparing data due to multiple systems that use different classification systems? For example, a supplier may be classified as providing "office supplies" in the supplier management system, but their purchase orders may be categorized as "stationery products" in the purchase order system. This mismatch in classification systems makes it challenging to track the total spend on office supplies across the organization and identify cost-saving opportunities related to office supplies. This discrepancy in classification systems creates a barrier to effectively consolidate and analyze data. It becomes difficult to aggregate spend data accurately and understand the true costs associated with specific categories or suppliers. The lack of consistency hinders the identification of patterns or trends that could reveal opportunities for cost reduction or negotiation leverage.

To overcome this challenge, I realized the importance of mapping and aligning the classification systems used by different departments or systems. It would definitely require collaboration with stakeholders from both the supplier management and purchase order systems to establish a standardized classification framework. By mapping the categories used in each system and creating a common taxonomy, we will be able to ensure consistent classification across all procurement-related data.

Data Handling within cross-platforms

Cross-platform data integration poses a significant challenge for integrating procurement data. You might find in your organizations that procurement data is stored in various systems and platforms, such as ERP systems, supplier databases, contract management systems, and more. Each platform may have its own data formats, structures, and APIs, making it complex to harmonize and integrate data seamlessly. The challenge lies in bridging the gap between these disparate platforms and ensuring smooth data flow across systems. Data mapping, data transformation, and data reconciliation become critical tasks in cross-platform data integration.

Data in Unstructured formats

All data that does not exist in rows and column format is categorized as unstructured data, such as text and images, which lack a predefined structure. Dealing with this kind of data is a completely different challenge. It cannot be handled in the same way as neatly organized data found in Excel sheets or SQL databases.

You might be wondering why we need to deal with unstructured data. For instance, you may recall a task where you had to analyze your contracts, which are filled with complex clauses and terms that prove extremely difficult to categorize or quantify. Extracting meaningful insights and data from these contracts feels like an uphill battle. For example, one contract might contain a clause related to early termination fees, and the fee could vary from contract to contract depending on the supplier and the specific terms outlined. In such cases, we need a solution that can automatically extract and structure the relevant information from contracts, enabling seamless integration into our procurement systems. This not only saves time and effort but also provides the necessary insights to make informed decisions.

Data from Mergers & Acquisitions

Mergers and acquisitions inherently introduce complexities when it comes to data integration. One company could use a completely different procurement system, and their data could be stored in a different format altogether. Months of effort to map the data from the two systems to align the product and supplier classifications is required. Added to this we also encounter challenges like language barriers, like while describing PO's.

Data from Legacy system

Organizations are not built in a day. So is their data. Data evolves as the organization grows. Simultaneously, technology is also evolving. Data was once stored on local machines with a particular format. But as the volume of data increases, better technology tools to store our data are recognized – it is important that the data is moved from the legacy systems to integrate with the modern databases. Obviously, the aging systems that had been in use for many years, and its unique data format would present a significant obstacle when it comes to integrating data with newer systems. We would find ourselves spending countless hours manually cleaning up and converting the data to fit into the new systems. We also need to ensure that the information is in a compatible format and ready for integration.

Data governance

Data governance ensures that the data is standardized, consistent, and reliable across all systems and processes. However, implementing effective data governance practices for procurement data can be challenging due to the complexity and diversity of the data sources involved. It requires defining data standards, data ownership, data stewardship, and establishing data quality controls. Furthermore, data governance also addresses privacy and security concerns, ensuring that sensitive procurement data is protected and accessed only by authorized personnel. Compliance with regulations such as GDPR adds an additional layer of complexity to data governance efforts.

Establishing a robust data governance framework specifically tailored to procurement data is the need. This framework should encompass data policies, data governance roles and responsibilities, data quality controls, and privacy and security measures. It should also foster collaboration between procurement teams, IT departments, and data governance professionals to ensure alignment and adherence to data governance principles.

Data quality

Data quality is a critical challenge when it comes to data integration for procurement data. Procurement data is sourced from various systems, including supplier databases, transactional systems, and contract management platforms. However, these data sources may have inconsistencies, inaccuracies, or missing information, leading to poor data quality. Ensuring high-quality data is essential for effective procurement processes and decision-making. Poor data quality can result in incorrect supplier evaluations, inaccurate demand forecasting, and flawed contract management. It can also lead to delays, errors, and increased costs in procurement operations.

Organizations need to implement data quality measures such as data profiling, data cleansing, and data validation. This involves identifying and resolving data inconsistencies, removing duplicate records, and validating data against defined business rules and standards.

Data Volume

Data volume presents a significant challenge for data integration in procurement. We know that procurement data encompasses a wide range of information, including supplier records, transactional data, contract documents, and more. The sheer volume of data can be overwhelming, making it difficult to process and integrate efficiently. Given the large volumes of data, it can result in performance issues, increased storage requirements, and longer processing times. It would lead to delays in data integration, impacting the speed and agility of procurement processes.

We would need to invest in scalable infrastructure and data storage solutions that can handle the volume of procurement data. Implementing data compression techniques, data archiving, and data partitioning strategies can help optimize storage and improve data integration performance. Additionally, leveraging technologies like data virtualization and distributed processing frameworks to distribute the processing load across multiple systems and handle large data volumes more effectively.

9. Organizational Culture

Organizational culture is yet another significant challenge for data integration in procurement. The culture of an organization plays a crucial role in shaping how data is perceived, valued, and managed. Resistance to change and a lack of data-driven mindset can hinder the adoption of data integration initiatives. The procurement teams may be accustomed to working in silos, with limited collaboration and data sharing practices. Cultural barriers can also lead to a lack of trust in data quality and reluctance to rely on integrated data for decision-making. Inconsistent data entry practices and data governance issues may prevail in an organization with a weak data culture.

Organizations need to foster a data-driven culture that promotes transparency, collaboration, and accountability.

This involves promoting data literacy, providing training and resources to employees, and emphasizing the importance of data integrity and accuracy. Leadership support and effective change management strategies are essential in driving cultural change and encouraging adoption of data integration practices.

Alas – the data integration challenge can keep going on and on as this is one of the humongous task and lays foundation to the digital journey. And it is very obvious that overcoming these challenges requires a multifaceted approach. We need to initiate conversations with the IT department and senior management to highlight the limitations of discrete data and the detrimental impact it will have on procurement operations. Exploring options for upgrading or replacing the system, seeking a solution that would enable smoother data integration, real-time insights, and enhanced functionality is what is required. We now understood the challenges posed to integrate data – But what is the data that is available to integrate. Lets move on to the next chapter to explore all the various types of data available within the procurement landscape.

CHAPTER IV

Diverse Data Sources in Procurement

Data – a catchy word! But where is all this sitting? We all know that data is everywhere. It just depends on what we want to see. We find data on our local laptops, within teams (like sourcing, contracting, etc.), within procurement as a whole, within cross-functional departments in the organization, and much more outside the organization. So, what data am I going to use to make a difference? Is it the internal data, external data, or is it enough for us to rely on the data used by one team?

If we want to aim for transformation in procurement, it is definitely not enough for us to stick to one kind of data. We need to extend our wings beyond data within procurement teams to data within cross-functional departments (like finance, operations, supply chain). Finance data provides insights into budgets, expenses, and payments, giving us a clear understanding of the financial aspects of procurement. Operations data, on the other hand, offers valuable information on inventory levels, production metrics, and demand forecasting, helping us assess the operational aspects of procurement. This brings in a lot of insights based on data within the organization.

But organizations do not and cannot function in silos. We need to understand benchmarks and other related external market data. Therefore, data exploration has to extend further and relate internal data with other external data available in the market. Market data is a crucial external source that provides insights into price trends, demand patterns, and competition within the industry. By analyzing market data, we can make strategic procurement decisions, negotiate favorable pricing, and stay ahead of market trends. Lastly, regulatory data also plays a significant role in ensuring compliance and managing potential risks.

In this chapter let us analyze various kinds of data available within procurement, within the organization and external data that could influence in outcome driven innovations to kick start the journey of digital procurement.

Internal Data

First, let's deep dive into the internal data available within procurement. Although this may vary in each organization, we can explore the most probable scenario considering the standardization of multinational corporations (MNCs) these days. The wide range of data sources available in procurement both excites and overwhelms us.

We are often aware of the tremendous value that can be unlocked by leveraging data from these different sources. To ensure that we don't miss out on any opportunities, let's compile a detailed list of each data source and the advantages it can bring to the table. By thoroughly analyzing and understanding these data sources, we can harness their power to drive better outcomes for any organization within procurement. The goal behind exploring these data sources is to help digital experts enhance their domain knowledge of procurement.

Requisition Data

Requisition data is the information related to the products or services that the organization needs to procure. It includes details such as the quantity required, product or service description, delivery timelines, preferred supplier details, and cost estimates. This data is important for procurement because it helps in identifying the items that need to be purchased, the quantity required, and the estimated costs. This information is used to prepare purchase orders, negotiate with suppliers, and manage the procurement process.

Requisition data can be captured and stored in various ways. In some organizations, requisition data is manually entered into a requisition form, which is then routed to the procurement team for processing. In few other organizations, requisition data may be captured electronically through a procurement software system. The software may have features that allow employees to request products or services through an online portal, and the system can automatically route the requests to the appropriate approvers for processing. Once the requisition data is captured, it is stored in a central repository or database. This allows the procurement team to access the data when they need it, and it also helps in tracking the status of each requisition. The data can be analyzed to identify spending patterns, monitor compliance with procurement policies, and identify opportunities for cost savings. Requisition data is an important source of information for procurement, and it plays a critical role in managing the procurement process efficiently and effectively.

Purchase Orders

When a procurement team wants to purchase goods or services from a supplier, they typically initiate the process by creating a purchase order. The purchase order includes all the necessary information related to the order, including the item or service being procured, the quantity, the delivery date, and the agreed-upon price. Once the purchase order is created, it is typically sent to the supplier for acceptance. Once the supplier accepts the purchase order, they will fulfill the order and send an invoice to the procurement team. The procurement team will then match the invoice against the purchase order and verify that the goods or services have been received as per the purchase order's terms. All the information related to the purchase order, including the item description, quantity, price, delivery dates, and supplier information, is captured and stored in the organization's procurement system. This information is used for a variety of purposes, such as tracking orders, monitoring supplier performance, and managing inventory levels. The procurement system will typically have a database that stores all the information related to purchase orders. This database can be accessed by authorized personnel in the procurement team to view, edit, and analyze the data.

Organizations can store their purchase order data in various systems/software. Typically, one of the following systems is used to store the PO data.

- Enterprise Resource Planning (ERP) systems: ERP systems are software applications that integrate all aspects of a company's operations, including procurement, finance, supply chain, and human resources.

- Procurement software: Procurement software is specifically designed to manage procurement activities, including creating and managing purchase orders.
- Supply chain management systems: Supply chain management systems help organizations manage the flow of goods and services from suppliers to customers. These systems often include features for creating and managing purchase orders, and organizations can store their purchase order data in them.
- Electronic document management systems: Electronic document management systems (EDMS) allow organizations to capture, store, and manage electronic documents. Many organizations use EDMS to store their purchase order data.
- Cloud-based storage solutions: Cloud-based storage solutions such as Dropbox, OneDrive, or Google Drive can also be used to store purchase order data. These solutions provide a centralized location for documents that can be accessed from anywhere with an internet connection.
- Spreadsheets: While not a recommended solution due to limited functionality and the potential for errors, some small organizations would store their purchase order data in spreadsheets such as Microsoft Excel or Google Sheets.

Purchase Order
Vendor: ABC Corporation
Date: May 10, 2023
PO Number: PO-20230510-001

Ship To:
Acme Inc.
123 Main Street
Anytown, USA

Item	Quantity	Description	Unit Price	Total Price
1	100	Widgets	$10.00	$1,000.00
2	50	Gizmos	$20.00	$1,000.00

Subtotal: $2,000.00
Tax: $200.00
Total: $2,200.00

Sample Purchase Order

In this example, the purchase order includes information such as the vendor (ABC Corporation), the date of the order (May 10, 2023), and a unique PO number (PO-20230510-001). The "Ship To" section specifies where the items will be delivered. The body of the purchase order includes a list of items being ordered, along with the quantity, description, unit price, and total price for each item. At the bottom of the purchase order, there is a subtotal for the items, a tax amount, and a total amount due.

Invoices

Invoices are an essential component of the procurement process as they contain vital information about the products or services purchased, the price, and payment terms. Invoices can be submitted by suppliers in paper or electronic format, depending on the organization's requirements. Invoices are crucial for accounting and financial purposes, and organizations must ensure that they are properly processed, verified, and recorded in the system. Accurate and timely invoice processing can help organizations avoid late payment penalties, maintain positive relationships with suppliers, and ensure compliance with various accounting and tax regulations.

Once an invoice is received, it needs to be processed, verified, and recorded in the system. The invoice processing workflow typically involves several steps, including matching the invoice with the corresponding purchase order and goods receipt, verifying the accuracy of the invoice data, and obtaining approval for payment.

Invoices are stored in various formats, depending on the organization's systems and processes. Some organizations may choose to store paper invoices in physical files, while others may scan and store them in digital formats. Electronic invoices can be stored in different formats such as PDF, XML, or EDI, depending on the supplier's invoice submission method and the organization's systems. The storage location of invoices can vary depending on the organization's systems and processes. Invoices can be stored in an Enterprise Resource Planning (ERP) system, a document management system, or a procurement system. The invoices may be stored in a central repository or distributed across different departments or business units.

ABC Company
123 Main Street
Anytown, USA 12345
Invoice # 12345

To: XYZ Inc.
789 Market Street
Othertown, USA 67890

Date: May 1, 2023

Description	Quantity	Price	Total
Product A	10	$50.00	$500.00
Product B	5	$75.00	$375.00
Shipping and handling			$25.00
Total		$900.00	

Payment Terms: Net 30 days

Thank you for your business!

Sample of a typical Invoice

Here, ABC Company is sending an invoice to XYZ Inc. for products (Product A and Product B) and services rendered (shipping and handling). The invoice includes a description of the products and services, the quantity, unit price, and total price for each item, as well as the total amount owed. It also includes the payment terms, which specify that the invoice must be paid within 30 days of the invoice date.

Contracts

Contracts are legal documents that outline the terms and conditions of an agreement between two or more parties. In procurement, contracts are used to establish the terms of the business relationship between a company and its suppliers. The information contained in contracts is critical to the procurement process as it outlines the scope of work, pricing, delivery schedules, quality requirements, and other key terms.

Capturing contract data involves several steps. First, the contract needs to be created, either by the company's legal department or by a procurement professional. During the contract creation process, all relevant information needs to be included, such as the scope of work, pricing, and delivery schedules. Once the contract has been created and approved, it needs to be signed by both parties. The signed contract then needs to be stored in a secure location for future reference.

Organizations use different methods to store contract data, depending on their preferences and requirements. Following the old school method some companies store contracts in hard copy format in filing cabinets, while others prefer to store them electronically in a document management system. A document management system allows for easy storage, retrieval, and sharing of contract data with relevant stakeholders.

To ensure that contract data is accurate and up-to-date, companies need to establish processes for managing and updating contracts. This involves regularly reviewing contracts to ensure that all obligations are being met and that pricing and other terms remain current. Regular contract reviews also help to identify any areas where changes may be necessary, such as when new products or services are added to the contract.

Supply Agreement

This Supply Agreement ("Agreement") is entered into as of [DATE] (the "Effective Date") by and between [SUPPLIER NAME], with its principal place of business at [ADDRESS] ("Supplier"), and [BUYER NAME], with its principal place of business at [ADDRESS] ("Buyer").

RECITALS

WHEREAS, Buyer desires to purchase certain goods (the "Goods") from Supplier;

WHEREAS, Supplier desires to sell such Goods to Buyer;

WHEREAS, the Parties desire to enter into this Agreement to set forth the terms and conditions of such sale and purchase of the Goods.

NOW, THEREFORE, in consideration of the mutual covenants and agreements herein contained, the Parties agree as follows:

TERMS AND CONDITIONS

1. Sale and Purchase of Goods

1.1. Supplier agrees to sell to Buyer and Buyer agrees to purchase from Supplier the Goods described in Exhibit A attached hereto (the "Goods") in accordance with the terms and conditions of this Agreement.

1.2. The purchase price for the Goods shall be as set forth in Exhibit A attached hereto.

2. Delivery

2.1. Supplier shall deliver the Goods to Buyer's designated delivery point(s) on the delivery date(s) specified in Exhibit A.

2.2. Buyer shall inspect the Goods upon delivery and notify Supplier within [NUMBER] days after delivery of any nonconformity or defect.

3. Payment

3.1. Buyer shall pay the purchase price for the Goods within [NUMBER] days after receipt of a proper invoice.

3.2. Invoices shall be submitted by Supplier to Buyer in accordance with the invoicing requirements set forth in Exhibit A.

4. Warranties and Representations

4.1. Supplier warrants and represents that the Goods shall conform to the specifications set forth in Exhibit A.

4.2. Supplier warrants and represents that the Goods shall be free from defects in material and workmanship.

5. Term and Termination

5.1. This Agreement shall commence on the Effective Date and shall continue until [DATE], unless earlier terminated in accordance with this Agreement.

5.2. Either Party may terminate this Agreement upon [NUMBER] days' prior written notice to the other Party.

6. Governing Law

6.1. This Agreement shall be governed by and construed in accordance with the laws of the State of [STATE].

IN WITNESS WHEREOF, the Parties have executed this Agreement as of the date first above written.

[SUPPLIER NAME]

By: ______________________

Name: ______________________

Title: ______________________

[BUYER NAME]

By: ______________________

Name: ______________________

Title:

A Typical Contract

This is a service agreement between ABC Corporation (referred to as "Client") and XYZ Services (referred to as "Service Provider"). The agreement outlines the terms and conditions under which the Service Provider will provide marketing services to the Client. The agreement covers the scope of work to be performed by the Service Provider, which includes developing and executing a marketing plan, conducting market research, and providing regular reports to the Client. The agreement also specifies the payment terms, with the Service Provider receiving a fixed monthly fee for their services. The contract includes provisions for termination, breach of contract, and confidentiality. It also specifies the governing law and jurisdiction in case of any disputes arising from the agreement. Both parties have signed the agreement, indicating their acceptance of the terms and conditions outlined in the contract. This contract serves as a legally binding document that outlines the rights and obligations of both the Client and the Service Provider in their business relationship.

Supplier Master Data

Supplier master data is an essential component of procurement activities as it forms the basis for managing supplier relationships. This type of data provides detailed information about suppliers, including their business profile, contact information, performance metrics, and product or service offerings. It helps procurement teams make informed decisions about which suppliers to work with, evaluate supplier performance, negotiate contracts, and manage the entire supplier relationship.

Typically, supplier master data includes the legal name, address, contact information, tax identification number, bank account details, and pricing history of the supplier. Additionally, it may include performance metrics such as delivery times, quality ratings, and other important information that is relevant to supplier selection and management. Procurement teams rely on this data to identify potential suppliers, evaluate supplier performance, and negotiate contracts that benefit both parties.

External sources of data, such as supplier ratings and reviews, industry benchmarks, and market intelligence, can be used in addition to collecting supplier performance data to gain a more comprehensive view of supplier performance. This information can be leveraged to identify opportunities for cost savings, mitigate risks associated with poor supplier performance, and make informed decisions about supplier selection and contract negotiation.

The process of capturing and storing supplier master data involves collecting information from various sources, including internal records, supplier websites, and public databases. This information is typically entered into a centralized database or enterprise resource planning (ERP) system. The data is then verified and updated on a regular basis to ensure accuracy and completeness. This ensures that procurement teams have access to up-to-date and reliable data to support their decision-making processes. Spend Data

Inventory Data

Inventory data is important to procurement because it helps in planning and managing the procurement process. By knowing the inventory levels, procurement professionals can make informed decisions about when and how much to order, ensuring that there is no overstocking or stockouts. Overstocking ties up capital and storage space, leading to unnecessary costs, while stockouts can lead to production delays and lost sales.

Moreover, inventory data helps in identifying the lead time for ordering products. The lead time is the time between the initiation of an order and the delivery of the products. By knowing the lead time, procurement professionals can plan for the procurement process, ensuring that the products are delivered on time and in the desired quantity.

Furthermore, inventory data also helps in managing supplier relationships. By monitoring inventory levels, procurement professionals can identify suppliers who consistently deliver products on time and in the desired quality, and those who do not. This information can be used to evaluate suppliers and negotiate better terms and pricing with the best-performing suppliers.

Inventory data can be captured and stored in various ways depending on the organization's size, complexity, and industry. In general, procurement teams rely on inventory management systems that provide real-time visibility into inventory levels, location, and movement.

- Use barcodes or radio frequency identification (RFID) technology to track inventory items. As items are received into inventory, they are labeled with a barcode or RFID tag that includes a unique identifier. Then, as items are moved or shipped, the tag is scanned to update the inventory records in the system.
- Use a warehouse management system (WMS) that can track inventory in real-time and optimize warehouse operations. A WMS can capture data on inventory levels, movement, and location through various methods such as manual scanning, voice commands, or automated conveyor systems.

- Cloud-based inventory management systems have become increasingly popular in recent years. These systems allow procurement teams to access inventory data from anywhere with an internet connection, collaborate with suppliers and other stakeholders, and automate many manual processes.

Procurement teams may also rely on spreadsheets, paper records, or other manual methods to track inventory levels. However, these methods can be prone to errors and may not provide real-time visibility into inventory levels, which can lead to stockouts or overstocking.

Product Name	Product Code	Quantity Available	Location
Widget A	A001	100	Warehouse 1, Aisle 2, Shelf 3
Widget B	B002	50	Warehouse 2, Aisle 1, Shelf 2
Part C	C003	500	Warehouse 1, Aisle 3, Shelf 1

Inventory Data

This inventory data provides information about the available quantity of different products in different locations within the warehouse. This information can be used by procurement to determine when to order more of a particular product, how much to order, and from which supplier. It can also help procurement plan production schedules and ensure timely delivery of products to customers.

Delivery Data

Delivery data is crucial for procurement as it allows organizations to track the status and location of goods during the shipping process. This data helps to ensure timely delivery of goods and identify any delays or issues that may arise during the transportation process. Capturing delivery data begins with the supplier providing a shipment notification, which includes information such as the carrier, tracking number, and expected delivery date. As the goods are transported, additional information such as pickup and delivery times, transit time, and any delays or exceptions are tracked and recorded.

Delivery data can be captured through various means, such as electronic data interchange (EDI) transactions, carrier tracking systems, or transportation management systems (TMS). Once captured, the data can be stored in a central database or integrated into a procurement platform for easy access and analysis.

Quality Control Data

Quality control data is a critical aspect of procurement as it helps organizations ensure that the products and services purchased meet the required quality standards. This data includes information about the testing and inspection of products or services, as well as any quality issues that may arise during the procurement process.

From a procurement perspective, quality control data is used to manage supplier performance by tracking their compliance with quality standards and identifying any areas where improvements may be needed. This data helps procurement teams make informed decisions about which suppliers to work with and how to negotiate contracts that include quality metrics and performance incentives.

In addition to managing supplier performance, quality control data is also used to mitigate risks related to product quality. By monitoring the quality of products and services purchased, organizations can identify potential risks and take appropriate actions to address them. For example, if a supplier consistently delivers products that fail to meet quality standards, the organization may decide to terminate the relationship or renegotiate the contract to include stronger quality requirements.

Capturing and storing quality control data involves collecting information from various sources, such as inspection reports, testing results, and customer feedback. This data is typically entered into a centralized database or quality management system, which allows procurement teams to track supplier performance and identify any quality issues that need to be addressed. Regular monitoring and analysis of quality control data helps organizations ensure that they are receiving products and services that meet their quality standards, and that their supplier relationships are contributing to their overall business success.

Cross Functional Data

Financial Data

A main function in any organization that procurement leans on is the Finance department. This plays a crucial role in procurement activities as it provides essential information related to budgeting, cost control, and financial analysis. Here's an elaboration on the components of financial data and their significance in procurement:

- Budget Information: Budget information refers to the allocated funds or financial resources designated for procurement activities. This data includes details about the approved budget for specific projects, departments, or time periods. Sharing budget information with finance teams helps ensure that procurement activities align with the allocated funds, enabling proper financial planning and resource allocation.

- Cost Structures: Cost structures encompass the breakdown of costs associated with procurement processes. It involves analyzing and categorizing expenses such as direct costs (e.g., purchase prices, transportation costs) and indirect costs (e.g., overhead expenses, operational costs). By sharing cost structures with finance teams, procurement professionals can collaborate on optimizing costs, identifying cost-saving opportunities, and evaluating the overall financial impact of procurement decisions.

- Payment Terms: Payment terms define the agreed-upon conditions and timing for making payments to suppliers. This data includes information about due dates, payment methods, discounts, and penalties. Collaborating with finance teams on payment terms ensures that procurement activities align with cash flow management objectives, optimize working capital, and adhere to financial policies and regulations.

- Financial Performance Metrics: Financial performance metrics provide insights into the financial effectiveness and efficiency of procurement activities. These metrics can include indicators such as cost savings achieved, return on investment (ROI), cost avoidance, supplier payment performance, and other relevant financial benchmarks. Sharing financial performance metrics with finance teams facilitates performance monitoring, financial analysis, and the identification of opportunities for improvement within the procurement function.

External Data

This data that is not captured within an organization. We generally need to rely on third parties to provide us this type of authentic data.

- Market data: Information on market trends, pricing, and supply chain disruptions can help procurement teams anticipate potential risks and make strategic sourcing decisions.
- Regulatory data: Data on regulatory requirements and compliance standards can help procurement teams ensure that their sourcing practices align with legal and ethical guidelines.
- Industry data: Data on industry-specific metrics such as product quality and innovation can help procurement teams benchmark their performance against industry standards.
- Economic data: Information on economic indicators such as inflation, currency exchange rates, and interest rates can help procurement teams make strategic sourcing decisions.
- Demographic data: Data on population trends, geographic distribution, and cultural factors can help procurement teams understand the needs and preferences of their customers and suppliers.

- Weather data: Information on weather patterns and natural disasters can help procurement teams anticipate potential supply chain disruptions and plan accordingly.
- Social media data: Insights from social media platforms can help procurement teams understand consumer trends and preferences, as well as monitor supplier reputations.
- News and media data: Information from news and media outlets can help procurement teams stay informed about industry developments and emerging market trends.
- Research data: Data from academic and industry research can provide valuable insights into emerging technologies, market trends, and best practices in procurement.

CHAPTER V

Understanding Data by marrying the right match

Once all the internal procurement data is listed, to truly make use of it, we need to map it properly. Data mapping is the process of matching the data elements from one system to another in a consistent and organized way. It involves identifying the data elements that are shared between systems and establishing relationships between them, so that data can be accurately and efficiently transferred or integrated between systems. Data mapping is important because it helps to ensure data integrity and consistency, improves data accuracy and efficiency, and reduces errors and redundancies in data transfer. It also helps to streamline business processes, improve decision-making capabilities, and increase productivity by reducing the time and effort required to manually transfer or reconcile data between systems. In a procurement system, data mapping would involve identifying the data elements in the purchase order system and mapping them to the corresponding fields in the invoicing system. This allows the data to be seamlessly transferred between systems, ensuring that accurate and consistent data is maintained across the procurement process.

So how does data mapping look like? To start data mapping process, let us first identify the key data elements in each of the internal procurement systems. We could create a matrix to show the relationships between these data elements.

This would allow us to see which data elements were similar across multiple systems and which ones were unique to each system. But how do I make the matrix? Here are the list of the tools and techniques that can come handy for data mapping in the procurement process.

- Spreadsheets: Spreadsheets are a simple yet effective tool for mapping data. They can be used to create a table or matrix that shows the relationship between data elements.

- Flowcharts: Flowcharts are visual representations that show the flow of data through different systems. They can be used to identify gaps in data and to highlight areas where data might be duplicated or missing.
- Data mapping software: There are several software programs available that are specifically designed for data mapping. These programs can automate the process of mapping data and can identify any inconsistencies or errors in the data.
- Business process modeling tools: Business process modeling tools can be used to map out the entire procurement process, including the flow of data. This can help to identify areas where data might be lost or duplicated and can help to streamline the process.
- Data profiling tools: Data profiling tools can be used to analyze the quality of data and to identify any inconsistencies or errors. This can help to ensure that the data being used for procurement is accurate and reliable.
- Online tools that can be used for data mapping.

- Altova MapForce: This is a data integration and mapping tool that enables users to map data between any combination of XML, database, flat file, EDI, Excel, XBRL, and/or Web service, then transforms data instantly or autogenerates royalty-free data integration code for the execution of recurrent conversions. *https://www.altova.com/mapforce*
- FME Desktop: This is a powerful data transformation and mapping tool that supports over 400 different data formats. It offers a wide range of data mapping and integration capabilities, including support for complex data structures and workflows. *https://www.safe.com/products/fme/fme-desktop/*
- Informatica PowerCenter: This is an enterprise-level data integration and mapping tool that enables users to create data maps for complex data integration projects. It offers a wide range of features and capabilities, including support for real-time data integration and complex data transformations.
- Talend Open Studio: This is an open-source data integration and mapping tool that supports a wide range of data formats and integration scenarios. It offers a wide range of features and capabilities, including support for cloud-based data integration and real-time data processing. *https://www.talend.com/products/data-mapping/*
- SAP Data Mapping - *https://www.sap.com/products/data-mapping-transformation.html*
- MapAnything - *https://mapanything.com/solutions/mapanything-mapping*

Now, we can see the discrepancies and inconsistencies in procurement data. For example, certain suppliers were listed differently in the supplier master data compared to the purchase orders, making it challenging to accurately track and manage supplier relationships. Similarly, variations in product descriptions and codes across different data sources, such as inventory data, purchase orders, and invoices, created confusion within the procurement process and hindered the smooth flow of information.

To address these issues, we need to establish a standardized approach for data elements. This involves creating a comprehensive set of data definitions to ensure consistency across all systems. It requires developing a standardized naming convention for suppliers, products, and other key data elements, along with clear rules for data entry. By enforcing consistent and standardized data elements, we can eliminate confusion and facilitate seamless data integration and analysis.

Once the data elements are standardized, the critical task is mapping the data. This entails identifying the corresponding data elements in each system and establishing links between them. For example, linking the supplier's name in the purchase orders to the supplier's name in the supplier master data, ensuring accurate synchronization across different systems. This mapping process allows us to connect the dots and create a unified view of the procurement data, enabling effective analysis and utilization of the information.

By standardizing data elements and mapping data across systems, we can achieve data consistency and integrity, making it easier to analyze and leverage procurement data for decision-making purposes. It is a meticulous process that requires attention to detail, but it lays a strong foundation for effective data integration and management within the procurement function.

Data Element	Purchase Orders	Invoices	Contracts	Inventory Data	Spend Data	Requisition Data	Delivery Data	Supplier Master Data	Quality Control Data
Supplier ID	X	X	X	X	X	X	X	X	X
Product ID	X	X	X	X	X	X	X		X
Quantity	X	X	X	X	X	X	X		X
Price	X	X	X	X	X	X	X	X	X
Delivery Date	X		X	X	X	X	X		
Invoice Date		X			X		X		
Payment Date	X	X	X		X	X			
Location				X			X		

An Example of a Matrix during the Data Mapping Process

Note that this is just a sample matrix and the actual data elements may vary depending on the specific procurement systems used by the organization. The matrix shows which data elements are captured by each system and which ones are shared across multiple systems. This helps identify any potential data redundancies or inconsistencies that need to be addressed in order to create a unified and accurate view of procurement data.

At the end of this process, we are now able to consume and derive insights from the data. However, let's say we want to derive additional insights by combining this data with other features or databases. This would require a similar mapping process to integrate the new data and derive new insights. Unfortunately, this can be a manual and repetitive task.

In the next chapter, I will introduce you to the concept of a Data Lake, which aims to overcome such scenarios. The Data Lake provides a centralized and scalable repository where data from various sources can be stored in its raw format. It allows for flexible integration and analysis of data without the need for repetitive mapping processes. By leveraging the capabilities of a Data Lake, we can streamline the data integration process, improve efficiency, and enable easier exploration and extraction of insights from diverse datasets.

Stay tuned for the next chapter where we delve into the concept of Data Lake and its potential to enhance data integration and analysis within procurement.

CHAPTER VI

Methodical approach to handle Big Data – The Data Lake!

We are now aware of how the fragmented and scattered nature of our data sources makes it arduous to gain a holistic view of our procurement processes and make informed decisions. The need of the hour is a solution that can unlock the true potential of data and revolutionize the procurement landscape. But how do we put all our data into one place and access it? Well, in this era of cloud services, big giants like AWS, G-Cloud, or Azure offer a variety of options. Yes, this could be the go-to approach - storing all data on the cloud and accessing it as needed by all the procurement professionals. However, if I go ahead and dump all my data on the cloud as is, will it be useful for me to consume the data whenever I require it? No, in order to make data-driven decisions, we have already seen that it requires proper mapping of data flowing from one system to another. This means that it is not enough to simply put all the data in one place. The data needs proper processing so that it makes sense when consumed from various procurement systems. This demands a framework in place that caters to all the steps, right from data ingestion to data consumption. This is where the concept of a Data Lake can help us.

In simple words, you can envision a data lake as a centralized repository, a vast reservoir that can house all our procurement data in its raw and unprocessed form. To start with, it would be a sanctuary where structured and unstructured data can coexist harmoniously, dismantling the silos that impede data accessibility and integration. With a data lake at our disposal, we can effortlessly access cross-domain data from various departments within the organization. No longer will we struggle to connect data from finance, PMO, or supply chain departments. The once time-consuming and arduous task of data integration and consolidation will be significantly streamlined, potentially saving up to 50% of the build time.

A data lake would further eliminate the need to construct duplicate data objects in our enterprise data warehouse (EDW). Instead, we could dedicate efforts to building reusable use cases within the data lake, thereby creating a singular source of truth for procurement data. This approach would not only enhance data accuracy and consistency but also yield a tangible return on investment (ROI) by constructing reusable use cases that could benefit multiple teams and projects.

This is not all – data lake is not just a repository for data integration, but also a powerful platform for advanced analytics, including machine learning and artificial intelligence. With advanced analytics at our disposal, we could unlock hidden insights, identify patterns, and establish correlations within our procurement data. This would empower us to make data-driven decisions, optimize our procurement processes, and drive innovation within the department. Data lake is like the missing puzzle piece that would transform procurement. It would create a culture centered around data, where our decisions would be grounded in accurate, timely, and comprehensive insights.

In this chapter let us explore and comprehend what a data lake architecture looks like and what it could offer to any large organization. Since data lake is a concept that could be used in any domain, I would try to ensure that the architecture we discuss in this chapter is tailored specifically to the procurement domain.

Data Lake Architecture

A data lake architecture comprises several key elements that work together to provide a robust and scalable environment for data storage and processing. Let's analyze and assess each component layer by layer, envisioning how it would fit into our procurement-specific data lake architecture. To aid our understanding, we can sketch diagrams and create visual representations that illustrate the flow of data, the integration of different systems, and the interactions between various components. These visual aids will effectively communicate the intricate workings of the data lake.

At its core, any data lake consists of five layers, each catering to a specific function. We can imagine a data lake as a rainbow cake with one colored layer stacked on top of another. The bottom-most layer serves as the repository for dumping all the data coming in from various sources. As we move up to the topmost layer, we find data that is refined enough for consumption. Let's discuss each of these layers and see how our data gets refined as we ascend the ladder.

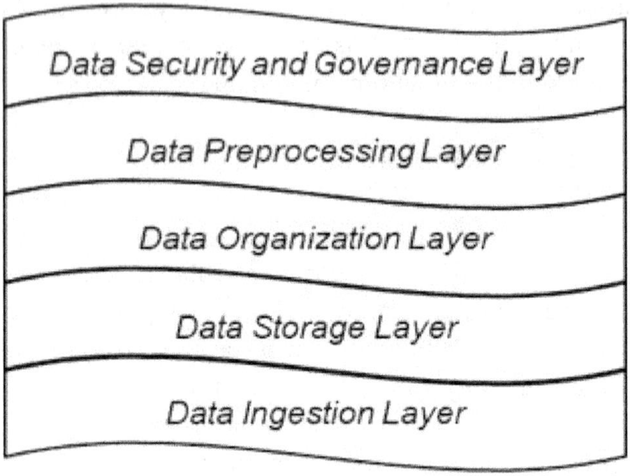

Data Security and Governance Layer

Data Preprocessing Layer

Data Organization Layer

Data Storage Layer

Data Ingestion Layer

A Typical Data Lake Layers

As you see in the diagram above, we will have a data ingestion layer as a base, followed by data storage layer, data organization layer, data preprocessing layer and a data security & governance layer. Let us now look at what role each of these layers would play in order to integrate procurement data.

Data Ingestion

In the context of a data lake, let's imagine you're going grocery shopping to cook a meal for a week. As you enter the supermarket, you refer to your shopping list or make smart choices based on your needs. This initial process of identifying and planning what to purchase represents the ingestion layer of the data lake, also known as the landing zone.

It is evident that data ingestion plays a pivotal role as the first and most crucial step in building our data lake. This process serves as the gateway to collecting data from diverse sources, both within and outside the organization. Data can originate from structured sources such as databases, spreadsheets, and enterprise systems, as well as unstructured sources like emails, documents, and social media feeds.

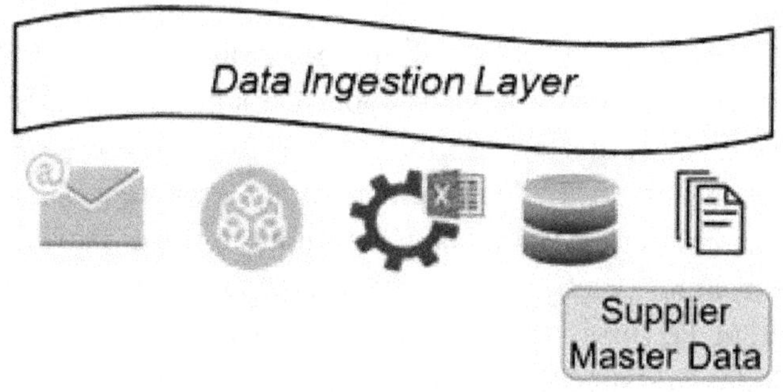

The Ingestion Layer

Understanding the significance of a well-designed data ingestion process is paramount in ensuring the efficient and accurate flow of data into the data lake. Data ingestion can occur in two ways: streaming and batch. Streaming ingestion involves processing and ingesting data in near real-time as it is generated, enabling immediate analysis and insights. This approach is particularly useful for scenarios requiring real-time event processing, continuous monitoring, or immediate action. Streaming ingestion ensures minimal latency between data generation and its availability for analysis. On the other hand, batch ingestion involves collecting and processing data in predefined intervals or batches. Data is accumulated over a specific period and then ingested into the data lake as a batch. Batch ingestion is suitable for scenarios where real-time analysis is not necessary, and data can be processed in larger chunks or at regular intervals. It allows for efficient processing of larger volumes of data and can be scheduled to align with business needs.

Data Storage

After completing your shopping, you gather all the groceries and load them into your car's boot. Similarly, in the data lake, this corresponds to the storage layer.

Data storage layer is a fundamental component of a data lake architecture. Data lakes commonly utilize distributed file systems, such as the Apache Hadoop Distributed File System (HDFS) or cloud-based storage solutions. These systems are specifically designed to handle large volumes of data while providing fault tolerance and scalability. Selecting the appropriate storage technology is crucial to effectively manage the ever-increasing data volumes and ensure reliable access to the data within the data lake.

The Storage Layer

There are various storage options available for data lakes, and the selection depends on factors such as data volume, velocity, variety, and the specific requirements of the organization. Some common storage technologies used in data lake architectures include:

- Distributed File Systems: Distributed file systems like the Apache Hadoop Distributed File System (HDFS) are commonly used in data lake environments. These file systems are designed to store and manage large volumes of data across a cluster of machines. They provide fault tolerance, high scalability, and efficient data processing capabilities.

- Cloud-based Storage Solutions: Cloud platforms offer scalable and cost-effective storage solutions for data lakes. Services like Amazon S3, Google Cloud Storage, or Microsoft Azure Blob Storage provide secure, durable, and highly available storage options. These cloud-based storage solutions are well-suited for storing and managing data at any scale, providing seamless integration with other cloud-based services and technologies.

- Object Storage: Object storage systems are designed to store unstructured data in a flat address space, where each piece of data is associated with a unique identifier. They provide high scalability, durability, and easy accessibility. Examples of object storage systems include Amazon Simple Storage Service (S3), Google Cloud Storage, and Azure Blob Storage.

- Columnar Databases: Columnar databases like Apache Cassandra and Apache HBase are optimized for storing and retrieving large volumes of structured and semi-structured data. They offer high scalability, efficient compression, and fast query performance, making them suitable for analytical workloads in data lake environments.

- Data Warehouses: Data warehouses, such as Amazon Redshift, Google BigQuery, or Snowflake, provide scalable storage and querying capabilities for structured and semi-structured data. These data warehousing solutions are designed to support high-performance analytics and ad hoc querying, making them ideal for data exploration and reporting in data lake architectures.

Data Organization

Just as you organize your groceries at home, categorizing items like dairy products in the refrigerator and dry goods on the shelves, the storage layer in the data lake ensures that data is stored and organized appropriately.

In a data lake, the data organization layer is responsible for structuring and organizing the data stored in the storage layer. This layer focuses on making the data more discoverable, accessible, and usable for various analytical and operational purposes. The data organization layer plays a crucial role in ensuring that data within the data lake is well-organized, governed, and easily accessible.

The Organisation Layer

Key activities that take place in the data organization layer of a data lake:

- Data Cataloging: Data cataloging involves creating a centralized inventory or catalog of all the data assets available in the data lake. It includes metadata management, which encompasses capturing essential information about the data, such as data source, schema, quality, lineage, and other descriptive attributes. The catalog serves as a searchable repository that helps users find and understand the available data assets.

- Data Categorization and Tagging: Data in the data lake is categorized and tagged based on different criteria, such as business domains, data types, data sources, or data sensitivity. Categorization helps in organizing the data based on its relevance to specific business areas or use cases. Tagging provides additional labels or attributes that can be used for data discovery and filtering.

- Data Governance: Data governance policies and practices are established in the data organization layer to ensure data quality, compliance, and security. This includes defining data standards, data classification policies, data access controls, and data lifecycle management. Data governance helps maintain consistency, integrity, and security of the data within the data lake.

- Data Lineage and Provenance: Data lineage refers to tracking the origins and transformations of data throughout its lifecycle. It captures information about the data's source, intermediate processes, and eventual consumption. Data lineage provides transparency and helps establish trust in the data, enabling users to understand how the data has been transformed and derived. Provenance adds another layer of information by capturing the history and context of data changes.

- Data Lake Optimization: The data organization layer may involve optimizing the data lake architecture for performance and efficiency. This can include techniques like partitioning, indexing, or compression to enhance data retrieval and processing speed. Optimization strategies aim to improve query performance, reduce storage costs, and provide an optimal balance between data access and resource utilization.

Data Processing

When it's time to cook, you collect the necessary ingredients from different areas of your kitchen and prepare them for cooking. This step aligns with the data preprocessing layer in the data lake. In this stage, the data is checked for quality, undergoes transformations, and is prepared to be consumed for various use cases.

In a typical data lake architecture, the data preprocessing layer follows the data organization layer. The data preprocessing layer focuses on preparing and transforming raw data to make it suitable for analysis and consumption by downstream applications and users.

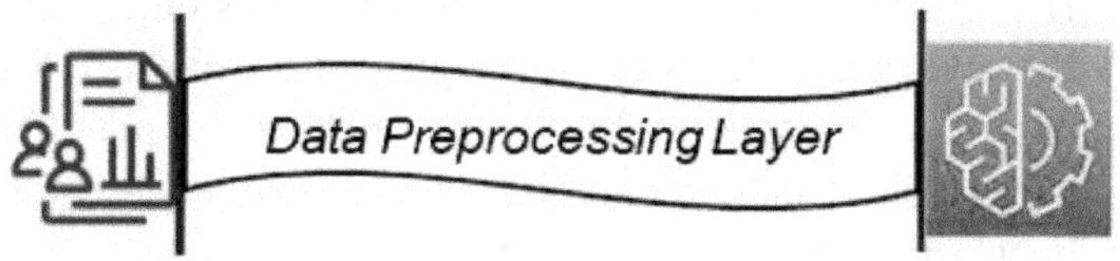

The Processing Layer

In the data preprocessing layer of a data lake, we would generally come across:

- Data Cleaning: Data cleaning involves identifying and handling data quality issues, such as missing values, inconsistencies, outliers, and errors. Various techniques, such as data imputation, deduplication, and outlier detection, are applied to clean the data and ensure its accuracy and completeness.

- Data Integration: Data integration involves combining data from multiple sources and integrating them into a unified and consistent format. This process may involve resolving schema differences, data format conversions, and data standardization to create a cohesive dataset that can be easily analyzed.

- Data Transformation: Data transformation includes applying various operations to convert the data into a more useful and structured format. This may involve aggregating data, performing calculations, deriving new variables, or applying statistical functions. Data transformation helps in creating features or attributes that are relevant for analysis or modeling.

- Data Enrichment: Data enrichment involves enhancing the existing data with additional information from external sources. This can include appending geographic data, demographic data, or market research data to provide more context and insights. Data enrichment helps in improving the depth and quality of the data for analysis.

- Data Validation: Data validation ensures that the preprocessed data meets specific criteria and adheres to predefined rules or constraints. This may involve performing data integrity checks, validating data against business rules, or verifying data consistency across different attributes or datasets.

- Data Sampling: Data sampling involves selecting a representative subset of data from the larger dataset for analysis or testing purposes. Sampling techniques, such as random sampling or stratified sampling, can be applied to extract a subset that retains the statistical properties of the original data.

- Data Formatting: Data formatting involves converting the preprocessed data into a specific structure or format suitable for analysis. This may include converting data into tabular formats like CSV or Excel, or formatting data into specific data models or schemas.

The output of the data preprocessing layer serves as a valuable input for downstream analytical processes and applications like Machine learning use cases.

Data Security and Governance

In a data lake, the data governance and security layer focus on implementing measures to ensure the security, privacy, and proper governance of the data stored within the data lake. This layer is responsible for establishing policies, procedures, and controls to protect the data assets and enforce compliance with regulations and organizational requirements.

The Security Layer

- Data Access Control: Data access control involves defining and enforcing access restrictions and permissions to ensure that only authorized individuals or applications can access and manipulate the data within the data lake. This includes implementing user authentication, authorization mechanisms, and role-based access control (RBAC) to manage user privileges and data access levels.
- Data Privacy and Compliance: Data privacy and compliance encompass ensuring that the data within

the data lake adheres to relevant privacy regulations and industry-specific compliance requirements. This involves implementing measures such as data anonymization, encryption, and data masking to protect sensitive information and prevent unauthorized disclosure or misuse of personal or confidential data.

- Data Classification and Metadata Management: Data classification involves categorizing the data within the data lake based on its sensitivity, importance, or regulatory requirements. This helps in defining appropriate security controls and access policies for different data types. Metadata management involves capturing and managing metadata, which provides information about the data's origin, structure, quality, and usage. Metadata helps in maintaining data lineage, understanding data dependencies, and ensuring proper data governance.

- Data Retention and Purging: Data retention policies specify the duration for which data should be retained within the data lake based on legal, regulatory, or business requirements. Data purging involves removing or anonymizing data that is no longer needed or exceeds the defined retention period. This helps in managing data storage costs, reducing data redundancy, and ensuring compliance with data retention regulations.

- Data Audit and Monitoring: Data audit and monitoring involve tracking and recording data access, usage, and modifications within the data lake. This helps in detecting and investigating any unauthorized or suspicious activities and maintaining an audit trail for compliance purposes. Data monitoring also includes real-time monitoring of data flows, system logs, and access patterns to identify any anomalies or potential security breaches.

- Data Quality Management: Data quality management focuses on ensuring the accuracy, completeness, consistency, and reliability of the data within the data lake. This involves implementing data quality checks, data profiling, data validation, and data cleansing processes to identify and rectify any data quality issues. Data quality management helps in maintaining the integrity of the data and ensures that reliable insights are derived from the data lake.

- Data Governance Framework: Establishing a data governance framework involves defining the organizational structure, policies, processes, and responsibilities for data management within the data lake. This includes roles such as data stewards, data owners, and data custodians who are responsible for ensuring data quality, compliance, and proper usage. The data governance framework provides guidelines and procedures for managing data throughout its lifecycle.

This layer plays a crucial role in building trust in the data lake and enabling secure and responsible data-driven decision-making.

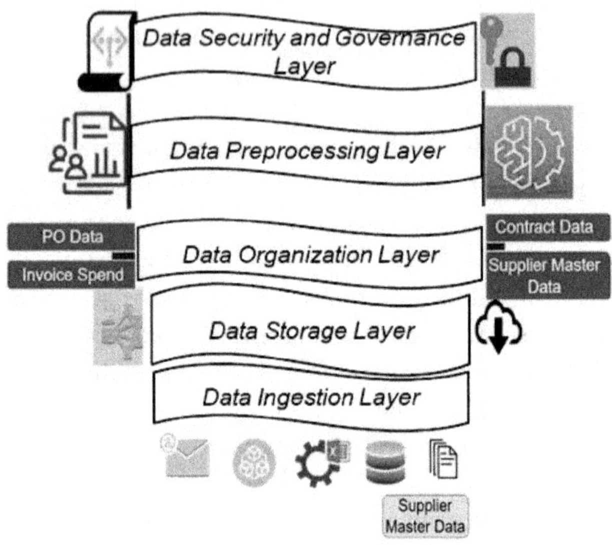

The Data Lake

CHAPTER VII

Takeaways - Part 1

Let us now wrap up on data integration in procurement, let us take a moment to reflect on the key points that were discussed. I will summarize this part of the book by emphasizing the following key takeaways:

- Data integration in procurement is a complex and time-consuming process that requires careful planning and execution. It involves combining data from various sources, both internal and external, to gain a comprehensive view of procurement activities.
- Data governance plays a critical role in ensuring the success of data integration. Establishing clear policies, procedures, and responsibilities for managing data throughout its lifecycle is essential to maintain data integrity, consistency, and security.
- Data quality is of utmost importance. Poor data quality can lead to inaccurate insights and flawed decision-making. Data cleansing, validation, and standardization processes are necessary to improve data quality and reliability.
- Collaboration and communication among stakeholders are vital for successful data integration. Procurement professionals need to work closely with IT teams, data analysts, and other relevant departments to address technical challenges and align goals.
- A well-designed data lake architecture provides organizations with the capability to unlock the value of their data, enabling advanced analytics, machine

learning, and data-driven decision-making. It fosters a data-driven culture within the organization, empowering users to explore, analyze, and derive meaningful insights from the vast data resources available.

By harnessing the power of data integration, procurement professionals can drive efficiency, streamline processes, and ultimately contribute to the organization's bottom line. I would encourage the readers to embrace data integration as a strategic imperative for procurement and leverage it as a valuable tool in their decision-making process. With this, I close this Part 1, excited to explore further aspects of data integration and its impact on procurement in the subsequent parts of the book.

Analytics Adventure

PART 2

"Data will talk to you if you're willing to listen."

- Jim Bergeson

CHAPTER VIII

Introduction to Procurement Analytics

It is an Aha!! moment - once you have accomplished the gigantic task of integrating all your data and accessing it seamlessly. A challenging yet rewarding task of building a central repository for all your data is planned and will be sorted out. This leads us to the next step of our journey. Yes, you have already guessed it – it is to leverage this data for data-driven insights to drive procurement excellence.

Procurement analytics, the art and science of extracting meaningful insights from procurement data, is the key to unlocking the untapped potential within organizations. The world of procurement analytics is vast, intricate, and filled with opportunities waiting to be discovered. It is time to take the leap and embrace the transformative power of data-driven insights in our pursuit of procurement excellence.

That said, it is not as straightforward as it seems. As you already know, it is not just about crunching numbers or generating reports; it is all about turning raw data into actionable intelligence. It is gaining a deeper understanding of our procurement processes, identifying areas for improvement, and making informed decisions that would drive cost savings and enhance supplier relationships. It is a strategic imperative for any organization looking to stay ahead in today's fast-paced, competitive business landscape. By harnessing the power of analytics, we could transform our procurement function from a reactive cost center to a proactive value driver. Yes - We can uncover hidden opportunities!!!

I've witnessed firsthand how data-driven insights can help shape procurement strategies, streamline operations, and fuel innovation. My research has helped me see how analytics can help us identify patterns, detect anomalies, and predict future trends. It has been a transformative experience, empowering me to make more informed decisions and collaborate effectively with stakeholders across the organization. To make this difference, we need to show something and build an effective story to communicate with our stakeholders. How do you show? Dashboards!! Let's explore the role of data visualization in procurement analytics and then see what various techniques and tools are available in the next chapter.

But what is it that we are trying to see in these visualizations? What is the foundation on which we are going to build up our data story? We need something that is measured at regular intervals – and that is nothing but our standard metrics. The impact these metrics could create when seen through a microscopic lens is the indicators that drive procurement performance. And based on this is how we build our data stories. So, be ready to explore the world of metrics and key performance indicators (KPIs) in Chapter 10. Some guidelines on how we could frame our problem statements to make the analytical dashboards more effective are discussed in the following chapter.

The analytics journey is a progressive one, starting from descriptive analytics, where we gain a comprehensive understanding of historical procurement data. This enables us to answer questions such as "What happened?" and "Why did it happen?". But the story does not end there. We move to diagnostic analytics, where we dive deeper into the root causes of procurement challenges and identify opportunities for improvement. As we progress further to Chapter 12, I will discuss predictive analytics, which empowers us to forecast future trends and outcomes. This will help us provoke thoughts to anticipate demand, optimize inventory levels, and mitigate supply chain risks. When we reach the tip of analytics, prescriptive analytics allows us to take proactive actions based on data-driven recommendations.

Before we conclude this part of the book, let us also spend some time understanding how we could build our initial dashboards. In the final chapter, I will walk you through the basics of dashboard development for descriptive and diagnostic analytics.

Together, let us embark on this transformative adventure, armed with data as our guiding light.

CHAPTER IX

Data Visualization

Almost every day, you come across YouTube ads emphasizing the importance of having data in a format that can be easily understood. We have all experienced how easy it is to read and comprehend Google Analytics, LinkedIn Analytics, or YouTube Analytics in comparison to raw data.

As procurement professionals, we often find ourselves overwhelmed by spreadsheets filled with rows and columns of numbers. However, with the help of visualizations such as charts, graphs, and infographics, we can grasp the essence of the data at a glance. This intuitive approach enables us to quickly identify trends, outliers, and correlations that might have otherwise gone unnoticed. For example, when analyzing supplier performance metrics, instead of going through lengthy spreadsheets containing multiple performance indicators, most of us have likely used visualizations such as line charts to track key metrics over time. This visual representation makes it easier to identify trends in supplier performance, such as variations in delivery times or fluctuations in quality ratings. By simply glancing at the chart, you can quickly pinpoint any outliers or areas that require attention, allowing you to take prompt action and address potential issues. By now, you are clear that visualizations help us enhance our ability to understand data.

Think of Google Analytics, which gives us the comfort of discovering patterns in the data with just a glance that would have remained invisible. Visualizations help in simplifying complex data through the use of interactive dashboards. We already know that dashboards can consolidate multiple data points into a single view, allowing us to explore different dimensions and filter data based on specific criteria. For instance, when analyzing spend data across different categories and suppliers, I can interactively select and filter the data to view specific subsets, such as spend by supplier or spend by category, or even drill down to individual transactions. This dynamic visualization not only saves time but also provides a comprehensive overview of procurement spend, enabling us to identify cost-saving opportunities, negotiate better contracts, and effectively manage our procurement budget. Although this is obvious, let us take a few baby steps to understand the basics before we dive in. Let's look at a simple example of how this dynamic visualization helps us.

Supplier	Category	Spend (USD)
Supplier A	Electronics	$10,000
Supplier B	Furniture	$8,000
Supplier C	Electronics	$5,000
Supplier B	Electronics	$6,000
Supplier A	Furniture	$7,000
Supplier C	Furniture	$4,500

Now, let's say we have an interactive procurement dashboard that visualizes the aforementioned data. The dashboard allows us to explore spend data across different dimensions and filter it based on specific criteria. For example, we can use the dashboard to analyze spend by supplier. By selecting Supplier A, we can see that their total spend is $17,000, comprising $10,000 in Electronics and $7,000 in Furniture. This visualization provides a clear picture of Supplier A's contribution to our overall spend and their distribution across different categories. Similarly, we can explore spend by category. By selecting the Electronics category, we can see a total spend of $21,000, with Supplier A accounting for $10,000 and Supplier B contributing $6,000. This insight allows us to understand the significance of each category in our overall spend and identify any category-specific trends or opportunities.

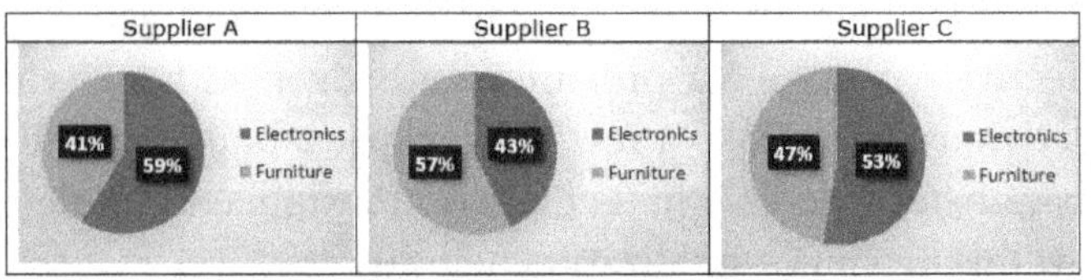

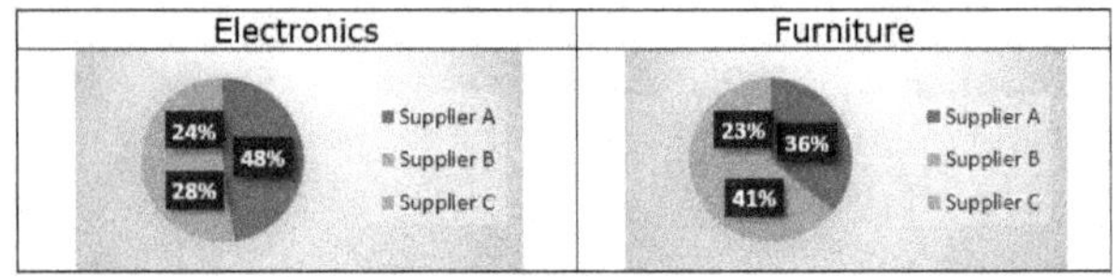

Furthermore, the interactive nature of the dashboard allows us to drill down into specific subsets of data. For instance, we can select Supplier B and further filter the data to view spend by category. This reveals that Supplier B's $8,000 spend is entirely attributed to the Furniture category. This granular view helps us understand the supplier's specialization and potentially negotiate more favorable terms or explore alternative suppliers for the Electronics category.

So, this interactive approach of exploring the data through the dashboard can help us identify cost-saving opportunities and make informed decisions. For example, we may notice that Electronics is a high-spending category with significant spend concentration among suppliers. This insight can guide us in negotiations to obtain better pricing or explore supplier consolidation strategies.

In addition to simplifying data, data visualization also helps uncover hidden patterns and correlations within the data. For instance, when examining the relationship between supplier pricing and quality ratings, a scatter plot can reveal whether there is a direct correlation between these variables. By plotting supplier pricing on the x-axis and quality ratings on the y-axis, I can visually assess if there is a pattern or cluster of data points indicating that higher-priced suppliers tend to have better quality ratings. This insight allows me to make data-driven decisions when selecting suppliers and negotiate contracts that balance both cost and quality. Let's take an example and examine this in detail.

Supplier	Pricing ($)	Quality Rating
Supplier A	100	8.5
Supplier B	120	9.2
Supplier C	80	7.8
Supplier D	110	8.9
Supplier E	90	8.2

Let's consider a simple data sample. We have a list of suppliers along with their respective pricing and quality ratings. To visualize the relationship between supplier pricing and quality ratings, we can create a scatter plot. In this plot, the pricing values will be plotted on the x-axis, and the quality ratings will be plotted on the y-axis. Each supplier will be represented by a data point on the scatter plot, enabling us to visually assess any correlation between these variables.

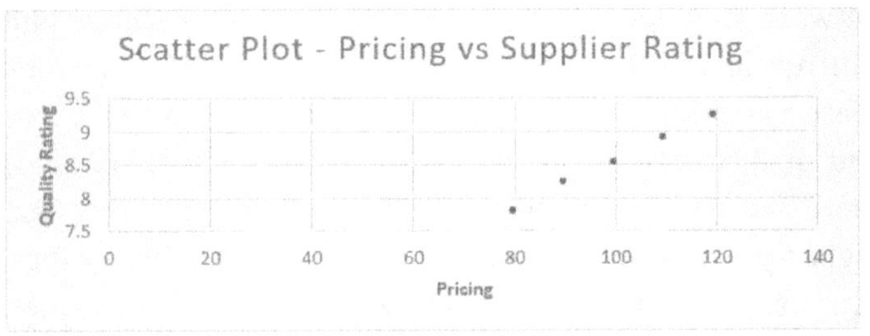

By analyzing the scatter plot, we can look for patterns or clusters of data points. For instance, if we observe that the data points tend to form an upward trend or cluster towards the upper-right corner of the plot, it suggests a positive correlation between higher pricing and better-quality ratings. Conversely, if the data points are scattered with no clear pattern, it indicates that there might not be a significant relationship between pricing and quality. Using this visualization, we can gain insights into the trade-off between supplier pricing and quality ratings. It helps us identify suppliers who provide better quality at higher prices or those who offer competitive pricing without compromising on quality. With this information in hand, we can make data-driven decisions in selecting suppliers and negotiating contracts that strike the right balance between cost and quality.

In a nutshell, data visualization helps us enhance data understanding, uncover insights and patterns, communicate complex information, and support decision-making.

Techniques and tools

Now, to leverage the full potential of data visualization in procurement analytics, it is crucial to explore and understand the various techniques and tools available. In our day-to-day work, we often find ourselves immersed in a sea of spreadsheets and data tables, attempting to make sense of the vast amount of procurement data. Despite our best efforts, it can be a daunting task to extract meaningful insights from rows and columns of numbers. We are in search of a better way to understand and present this wealth of information. It is clear that relying solely on data in rows and columns is no longer sufficient. Therefore, we are on the verge of discovering new techniques and tools that can help us harness the true power of our data.

Visualization techniques in procurement analytics encompass a range of approaches that can effectively represent and analyze procurement data. You may already be using many of the techniques listed here as part of your day-to-day job. However, the intention here is not to introduce these common techniques, but rather to compile them in one place. Additionally, let us explore how these techniques can be applied to different types of procurement data.

Charts and Graphs

- Bar Charts: I personally feel that a bar chart is one of the simplest and most comprehensible charts. You have likely used it numerous times. It is highly suitable for comparing quantities or values across different categories of procurement data. For example, you can use it to compare spend amounts across different suppliers or categories.

- Line Charts: These are also simple charts that are ideal for tracking trends and changes over time. They can be used to visualize the variation in procurement costs or supplier performance over different time periods.

- Pie Charts: When I need to display the proportionate contribution of different elements to a whole, a pie chart is the one I choose. This visualization makes it very easy to comprehend the role of a part with respect to the whole. For instance, it can be used to visualize the distribution of spend across different categories. We have previously used this to depict the spend across various suppliers and categories in the previous section.

Diagrams and Flowcharts

- Process Flowcharts: These are effective for mapping and visualizing procurement processes, showing the sequential steps involved and potential decision points. They allow us to identify the points where problems arise and help us analyze them. I will provide in-depth information on how we do this in Chapter 4. A sample of how a procurement process flowchart looks is shown in the figure below.

Typical Procurement Process Flow

- Decision Trees: Helpful for representing decision-making processes, where different procurement options or paths can be visually depicted based on certain criteria or conditions. This decision can be made by human intelligence if the number of decision points is few. However, if there are numerous dimensions involved, it is advisable to utilize machine learning techniques to build a more robust decision tree.

Maps

Geographic Heatmaps: Ideal for visualizing geographical distribution and variations in procurement data, such as supplier locations or procurement spend across different regions.

Infographics

Like the popular advertisement saying goes, "add color to life," infographics add essence to what we want to convey. By utilizing icons, illustrations, and concise text, infographics can effectively communicate key procurement metrics and insights in a visually appealing and easily understandable format. Infographics combine various visualization elements, including charts, graphs, icons, and text, to present a comprehensive view of procurement data. They are useful for summarizing key metrics, trends, or insights in a visually appealing and engaging manner.

Infographics

However, it wasn't just about the techniques; I also recognized the importance of finding the right tools. I explored popular visualization tools such as Tableau, Power BI, and QlikView. These platforms offered a range of features, from interactive dashboards to drag-and-drop interfaces, enabling me to transform our raw data into compelling visualizations.

Below is a table that provides an overview of the features and licensing options available with these tools for reference. Please note that the selection of the appropriate tool depends on the organization's specific needs and requirements. It is essential to conduct a thorough investigation of the various advantages and disadvantages that each tool offers before making a decision.

Tool	Advantages	Disadvantages	Licensing Options
Tableau	➤ Intuitive and user-friendly interface ➤ Robust data connectivity options ➤ Wide range of visualizations	➤ Costly for enterprise-level licenses ➤ Steeper learning curve for advanced features ➤ Limited collaboration capabilities	Per-user, Creator, Explorer, Viewer, and Tableau Online
Power BI	➤ Seamless integration with Microsoft ecosystem ➤ Affordable pricing options ➤ Strong data modeling features	➤ Limited customization options compared to other tools. ➤ Limited chart types and formatting options	Per-user, Pro, Premium, and Power BI Embedded
QlikView	➤ Associative data model for dynamic data exploration ➤ Rapid application development ➤ Excellent scalability	➤ Steeper learning curve for beginners ➤ Limited visualization options compared to other tools	User-based, Document-based, and Analyzer-based

Comparison between Visualisation Tools

While these tools are helpful in building your final dashboards, it is also important to have visualizations during the interim stages of developing a solution. Python libraries such as Matplotlib and Seaborn provide user-friendly interfaces and robust functionalities for designing and customizing visualizations using programming skills. If you are a data scientist reading this, I am sure you will appreciate the capabilities that these libraries offer when building a proof of concept.

After careful evaluation and testing, it is crucial to find the perfect combination of techniques and tools that align with our procurement needs. Once again, the choice of visualization technique should align with the goals of your procurement analytics and the type of insights you aim to extract from the data.

We have explored different visualization techniques and tools, but the question arises: what do we visualize? In order to effectively visualize data on dashboards, we need to establish some standard metrics and key performance indicators (KPIs). These metrics and KPIs will serve as the foundation for our visualizations and help us track the performance and progress of our procurement processes.

To delve deeper into defining these metrics and KPIs, let's move on to the next chapter. There, we will explore the essential elements that need to be considered and defined in terms of metrics and KPIs to drive our procurement analytics and visualization efforts.

CHAPTER X

What do we measure?

As a procurement professional, you recognize the significance of metrics and key performance indicators (KPIs) in assessing and improving procurement activities. The ability to measure and track performance is crucial for strategic decision-making and achieving desired outcomes. In this chapter, we will explore the world of standard metrics, KPIs, and success metrics in procurement, uncovering their valuable insights and impact on continuous improvement.

The first step in evaluating procurement performance is defining standard metrics. These metrics serve as benchmarks for assessing various aspects such as cost savings, supplier performance, contract compliance, and purchase order cycle time. By adopting standardized metrics, organizations can streamline evaluation processes and gain a clear understanding of areas for improvement.

While standard metrics provide a foundation, they may not capture the complete picture of procurement effectiveness. This is where KPIs come into play. KPIs are specific metrics aligned with strategic objectives, offering actionable insights into performance. Tailored to an organization's goals, priorities, and industry requirements, KPIs allow organizations to focus on critical success factors and make informed decisions to drive performance improvement.

Throughout this chapter, we will explore examples of commonly used standard metrics, including cost savings, supplier performance, contract compliance, purchase order cycle time, and inventory turnover. Additionally, we will delve into the significance of KPIs, which are specific, measurable, and time-bound metrics providing insights into the achievement of strategic objectives.

By the end of this chapter, you will have a comprehensive understanding of the role of standard metrics and KPIs in procurement, along with their relationship. Equipped with this knowledge, you will be able to define and implement these metrics within your organization, effectively measure performance, identify areas for improvement, and drive success in procurement operations.

Standard metrics

Standard metrics in procurement refer to the essential measurements used to monitor and evaluate various aspects of procurement activities. These metrics provide a quantitative assessment of performance and enable organizations to track progress, identify trends, and benchmark against industry standards. Standard metrics often encompass a wide range of areas within procurement, including spend analysis, supplier performance, contract management, savings realization, and risk management. By defining and consistently monitoring these metrics, procurement teams gain a comprehensive understanding of their performance and can identify areas for improvement.

To start, let's focus on defining standard metrics in procurement. These metrics serve as foundational measures that are commonly used across organizations to track and assess procurement performance. Some examples of standard metrics include:

1. Total Cost Savings: This metric measures the overall cost savings achieved through procurement initiatives, reflecting the success of cost reduction efforts.
2. Supplier Quality Index: This metric evaluates the performance of suppliers based on quality ratings, ensuring that high-quality products and services are consistently delivered.
3. Procurement Cycle Time: This metric tracks the time it takes to complete the procurement process from requisition to purchase order, aiming to streamline and improve efficiency.
4. Spend Under Management: This metric represents the percentage of spend that is actively managed by procurement, indicating the level of control and influence over purchasing activities.
5. Contract Compliance: This metric measures the extent to which suppliers adhere to contractual terms and conditions, ensuring compliance with established agreements.

Key Performance indicators (KPIs)

KPIs are a subset of metrics that are carefully selected to reflect the most critical aspects of procurement performance. KPIs are strategic metrics that are aligned with organizational goals and objectives. They provide a focused and actionable view of performance and enable organizations to measure progress towards specific targets. KPIs serve as key indicators of success and are used to monitor performance, drive improvement initiatives, and make informed decisions. KPI's could further be classified depending on what you are indicating – like the operational

KPI's, Performance KPI's, efficiency KPI's.

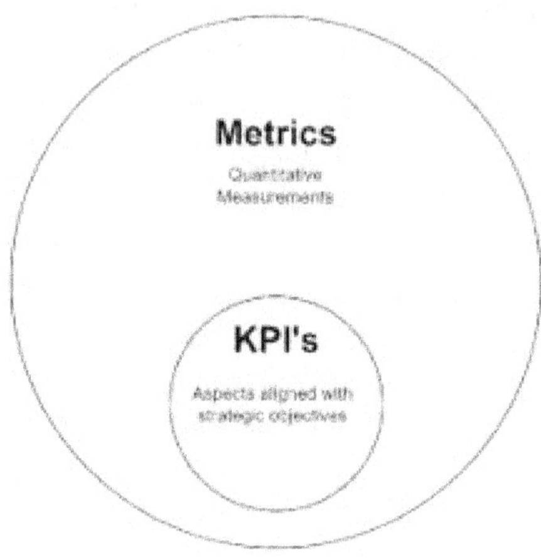

Standard Metrics vs KPI's

In this Venn diagram, the two circles represent "Metrics" and "KPIs," with their overlapping area representing the common ground between the two. The circle labeled "Metrics" represents the quantitative measurements used to evaluate and track various aspects of procurement performance. These metrics provide specific data points, such as cost savings, spend analysis, supplier performance, and cycle times.

The circle labeled "KPIs" represents the subset of metrics that are selected as key performance indicators, reflecting the most critical aspects of procurement aligned with strategic objectives. These KPIs are strategic indicators that guide decision-making and provide a focused view of operations, performance and efficiency. The overlapping area between the two circles represents the metrics that serve as both quantitative measurements and key performance indicators. These are the metrics that have been identified as critical to monitor and drive strategic procurement outcomes.

Once standard metrics are established, organizations can further refine their measurement approach by defining KPIs. KPIs provide a focused and targeted assessment of performance in areas that directly contribute to organizational success. They are carefully selected to align with the organization's strategic priorities and are tied to specific outcomes or desired results. KPIs help procurement professionals to measure progress, set targets, and drive performance improvements.

KPIs:

1. Cost Savings Ratio: This KPI calculates the percentage of cost savings achieved in relation to the total spend, providing a clear indicator of cost optimization efforts.
2. Supplier Performance Scorecard: This KPI combines multiple metrics, including on-time delivery, quality ratings, and responsiveness, to assess overall supplier performance and identify areas for improvement.
3. Procurement ROI: This KPI measures the return on investment generated through procurement activities, demonstrating the financial impact of effective procurement strategies.
4. Purchase Order Cycle Time: This KPI focuses on the time it takes to process and approve purchase orders, aiming to reduce delays and enhance procurement agility.
5. Supplier Diversity Index: This KPI evaluates the diversity and inclusivity of the supplier base, reflecting the organization's commitment to promoting supplier

diversity and social responsibility.

Aligning with organizational goals

We have defined our standard metrics and KPI's in the previous section. We are now set and understand what the difference between the standard metric is and a KPI. But now, it is important to see that all our metrics and KPI's are aligned with the organizational objectives.

Every organization has some set goals. We need to understand the importance of aligning procurement metrics and KPIs with organizational objectives to drive strategic outcomes. Let's consider an example to demonstrate this alignment:

Organization Objectives:

Objective 1: Achieve cost savings and cost optimization.

Objective 2: Ensure supplier performance and quality.

Objective 3: Enhance procurement efficiency and process effectiveness.

Well, the goal of defining these metrics is to provide a common language and set expectations for procurement professionals, stakeholders, and suppliers, ensuring alignment with organizational goals and objectives. But the question is how we measure the metrics and KPI's that we have defined above. They are not measurable. How will I know that I have achieved or near to achieve my organizational goals. Let us attempt to redefine our metrics and KPI's by having a measurable metric. But in order to do this it is also important that we also should have a benchmark with respect to our organization objectives.

So, let us now define the organization objectives with certain benchmarks:

Organization Objectives:

Objective 1: Achieve a 10% cost savings on total spend.

Objective 2: Maintain a supplier quality rating of 95% or above.

Objective 3: Reduce the procurement cycle time by 20%.

Aha!! The objectives remain more or less the same – but now I have a number/measure.

Based on the above objectives, let us redefine our standard metrics which we defined in the previous section:

1. Total Cost Savings: Target of **$1 million** in cost savings achieved through procurement initiatives.
2. Supplier Quality Index: Maintain a supplier **quality rating of 97%.**
3. Procurement Cycle Time: Reduce the procurement cycle time from 20 days to 16 days.
4. Spend Under Management: Aim to have **90% of total spend** actively managed by procurement.
5. Contract Compliance: Maintain a contract **compliance rate of 90%** or above.

Look, though they remain the same as per definition, we have very clearly mentioned on what we need to measure. Let us also redefine our KPI's accordingly.

1. Cost Savings Ratio: Achieve a **cost savings ratio of 12%.**
2. Supplier Performance Scorecard: Maintain an overall supplier performance score of **90%** based on a combination of quality, on-time delivery, and responsiveness metrics.
3. Procurement ROI: Aim for a procurement **ROI of 15%,** indicating the financial impact generated through procurement activities.

4. Purchase Order Cycle Time: Reduce the average purchase order cycle time **from 10 days to 8 days**.
5. Supplier Diversity Index: Maintain a **supplier diversity index of 0.5**, indicating a diverse supplier base.

By setting specific targets and aligning these metrics and KPIs with the organization's objectives, you can effectively track and measure the performance of procurement initiatives. These numbers provide a realistic framework to monitor progress and drive continuous improvement in procurement operations.

CHAPTER XI

Definition of Problem Statement

We have data that is well-organized after integration. We have recognized the importance of visualization, and we are now aware that there are many techniques and tools available to build our visualizations. Additionally, we all agree that defining KPIs is necessary to display them on the visualization tool. These KPIs, when combined, form a story that we are targeting. This story represents the problem that we aim to solve. Clearly defining the problem is the basis of analytics.

The success of the iPhone was not a result of magic but rather its ability to address multiple problems that existed at the time. When the iPhone was initially released, it did not even have a video option. Despite its minimalistic features, it became a huge success. On the other hand, it was also exorbitantly priced. The first iPhone, released in 2007, was priced at $499, which is equivalent to $645 in today's currency. The pricing of the most expensive BlackBerry devices during that time ranged from around $200 to $400, depending on the features and specifications of the device. So, what made the iPhone such a massive hit?

The key to the iPhone's success was its ability to solve a variety of problems faced by users. It combined the functionality of a mini-computer for checking official emails with the popular entertainment features of the iPod into one cohesive system. The problem statement was clearly defined, and the focus was on understanding the customers' needs and challenges. Developing a solution around this problem statement involved a strategic process.

Setting up a problem statement requires careful consideration of several important factors. By keeping these factors in mind, we can ensure a well-defined problem statement. This allows us to effectively address the specific needs and challenges faced by customers.

In this chapter, I will share my insights and experiences regarding the process of defining a problem statement in procurement analytics. This crucial step sets the foundation for effective data analysis and ensures that the analytics efforts are aligned with the desired outcomes.

Understanding the Problem

The process of defining a problem statement begins with gaining a deep understanding of the procurement landscape and the challenges faced by the organization. By thoroughly analyzing the current state of procurement operations, supplier relationships, and key performance indicators, we can identify areas that require improvement or optimization. This understanding helps us pinpoint the specific problem or opportunity that needs to be addressed through data analysis.

One approach to understanding the problem is by visualizing the procurement process and analyzing its flow. By examining each step in the process, we can identify potential bottlenecks or areas of delay. For example, if we observe a delay in the approval process, we can delve into the data associated with that step and investigate the reasons behind the delay. This analysis allows us to envision the future state we aspire to achieve and identify the gap between the current state and the desired state, which forms the basis of the problem statement.

Additionally, conducting a root cause analysis is crucial in defining the problem accurately. Often, the initial problem statement is a symptom of an underlying issue. Using techniques such as the "5 Whys," we can dig deeper and uncover the root cause. This involves repeatedly asking "why" until we reach the underlying cause of the problem. Understanding the root cause helps us identify the right data sources and approaches to solve the problem effectively.

For instance, suppose you encounter an issue where your inbox is not refreshing, preventing you from accessing your emails. Initially, you may think that calling the IT help desk is the solution. However, by applying the "5 Whys" technique, you realize that the root cause of the problem is a faulty router. The problem statement of "My inbox is not refreshing" is actually solved by "buying/replacing the router" rather than simply calling the IT help desk.

Understanding the root cause of the problem enables us to identify the appropriate data sources and solutions to address the issue effectively.

Stakeholder Engagement

Engaging with key stakeholders is an integral part of the process of defining the problem statement. It is important to involve not only data management and IT professionals but also procurement professionals, senior management, and other relevant stakeholders. This collaborative approach allows us to gain valuable insights into their perspectives, priorities, and pain points. After all, these stakeholders will be the end users of the digital solution.

By involving stakeholders from different areas of the organization, we ensure that the problem statement accurately reflects the needs and expectations of all parties involved. This collaborative effort leads to a more comprehensive and impactful analysis, as it takes into account the diverse perspectives and requirements of the stakeholders.

Defining the Objective

Once the problem has been identified, it is crucial to clearly define the objective of the analysis. What do we aim to achieve through procurement analytics? Are we looking to optimize supplier selection, reduce costs, improve supply chain efficiency, or enhance overall procurement performance? Defining a specific objective provides a clear direction for the analysis and helps prioritize the data and metrics to be examined. And definitely this objective has to be aligned with the overall objective of Procurement department.

Formulating Hypotheses:

In procurement analytics, formulating hypotheses plays a crucial role in defining the problem statement and guiding the analysis process. Hypotheses are educated guesses or assumptions about the relationship between variables or factors that may influence the problem or objective at hand. They serve as a starting point for data analysis and help in selecting the appropriate analytical techniques.

Let's consider an example to better understand the concept of formulating hypotheses in procurement analytics. Suppose we are analyzing the impact of supplier lead time on inventory levels. The problem statement is to identify the relationship between these two variables and determine if reducing lead time can help optimize inventory management.

Based on prior knowledge and experience, we can formulate a hypothesis such as:

"Hypothesis: A reduction in supplier lead time will result in lower inventory levels."

This hypothesis assumes that by decreasing the time it takes for suppliers to deliver goods, we can reduce the amount of inventory required to meet demand. It sets the direction for our analysis and guides us in exploring the data to validate or refute the hypothesis.

Next, we collect data on supplier lead times and corresponding inventory levels over a specified period. Using appropriate analytical techniques, such as regression analysis or correlation analysis, we analyze the data to determine if there is a significant relationship between supplier lead time and inventory levels.

If our analysis confirms a strong negative correlation between supplier lead time and inventory levels, it supports our hypothesis. This would suggest that reducing lead time can indeed lead to lower inventory levels, providing an opportunity for improved inventory management and cost savings. On the other hand, if the analysis does not find a significant relationship, it indicates that other factors may be influencing inventory levels, and we may need to explore alternative hypotheses or factors that contribute to the problem.

Iterative Refinement:

The process of defining a problem statement is not a one-time event but rather an iterative and evolving process. As we gather more insights, engage with stakeholders, and gain a deeper understanding of the problem, it is essential to refine and fine-tune the problem statement accordingly. This iterative approach ensures that the problem statement remains relevant, aligned with the changing dynamics of the procurement landscape, and addresses the most critical challenges.

CHAPTER XII

Diagnostic Analytics in Procurement

In this chapter, let's talk about the essential concepts and techniques that enable organizations to gain deep insights and identify the root causes of performance issues in procurement.

Diagnostic analytics goes beyond descriptive analysis and dives into the "why" and "what" behind the data, helping you make informed decisions and drive continuous improvement. Through diagnostic analytics, I can ask critical questions such as, "Why did a particular supplier fail to meet delivery deadlines?" or "What factors contribute to cost overruns in specific categories?" By answering these questions, you can immediately identify areas for improvement and take proactive measures to enhance procurement practices. By harnessing the power of diagnostic analytics, we can make data-driven decisions that address the underlying causes of performance issues and drive continuous improvement. This approach helps us move beyond simply reacting to problems and enables us to proactively identify areas of improvement, optimize costs, mitigate risks, and enhance our overall procurement performance. Rather than simply addressing symptoms of performance issues, we can dive deeper into the data to identify the true causes and take appropriate actions to drive positive change. This approach empowers us to optimize procurement processes, enhance supplier relationships, reduce costs, and mitigate risks.

The scope of diagnostic analytics in procurement is broad and covers various aspects of the procurement function. It involves analyzing data related to purchase orders, supplier performance, cost management, quality assessment, risk mitigation, and contract management – just to name a few. Additionally, diagnostic analytics can be applied at different levels within the procurement function. It can be used to analyze individual supplier performance, assess the overall performance of procurement categories, or evaluate the effectiveness of procurement strategies and policies. The scope of diagnostic analytics is not limited to a specific area or level but extends to the entire procurement ecosystem. Understanding the purpose and scope of diagnostic analytics is crucial for effectively applying this approach. In the following sections, we will explore the key components, techniques, and metrics associated with diagnostic analytics, providing practical guidance on its implementation in procurement processes.

Let us start by defining diagnostic analytics and exploring its purpose and scope within the procurement context.

Performing diagnostic analytics requires a combination of data collection, integration, and analysis techniques. Hopefully, by now, we are confident in integrating the data from different sources. With the help of advanced analytical tools and techniques, correlations and trends that provide valuable insights and patterns can be uncovered. We will explore various analytics techniques and tools, including descriptive analysis, root cause analysis, trend analysis, and comparative analysis in the next section. These techniques will enable you to uncover patterns, identify anomalies, and gain a comprehensive understanding of the underlying factors impacting procurement performance.

The chapter will then highlight the key metrics and KPIs used in diagnostic analytics, focusing on supplier performance, cost analysis, quality assessment, and risk management. These metrics serve as the foundation for uncovering insights and driving improvements in procurement processes.

At the end of this chapter, we will discuss the challenges associated with implementing diagnostic analytics and provide best practices to overcome these hurdles. Ensuring stakeholder buy-in, building analytical capabilities, and adopting an iterative approach will be explored as key success factors.

In a nutshell, this chapter will emphasize the significance of diagnostic analytics in procurement and its ability to drive data-driven decision-making, uncover insights, and foster continuous improvement.

Methodologies for Diagnostic Analytics

Are you ready to explore various techniques and tools that can be employed to conduct diagnostic analytics in procurement processes?

Root Cause Analysis

This technique aims to identify the fundamental reason behind a problem or anomaly. Most of the time, the root cause of the problem needs to be solved to address the issue effectively.

It involves systematically examining data, conducting interviews or surveys, and applying problem-solving methodologies such as the 5 Whys technique or fishbone diagrams.

Let's consider an example of contract delays in contract management. One way to tackle this problem is to examine the data. While examining the data, we can gather information related to contract timelines, approval processes, stakeholder involvement, and any other relevant factors. By analyzing this data, you can identify patterns or trends that may be contributing to the delays.

Furthermore, the company can conduct interviews or surveys with individuals involved in the contract management process, such as contract managers, legal teams, or procurement staff. Through these discussions, they can gather insights into potential bottlenecks, communication gaps, or challenges faced during the contract lifecycle.

We could also introspect the problem using the famous 5 Whys technique that we discussed in the previous chapter. Here's an illustration of how the 5 Whys technique can be applied to the problem of "contract delays":

Problem: Contract delays

1. Why are contracts getting delayed?

- Answer: Contracts are not being reviewed and approved on time.

2. Why are contracts not being reviewed and approved on time?

- Answer: The contract review process involves multiple stakeholders.

3. Why does the involvement of multiple stakeholders cause delays?

- Answer: There is a lack of clarity on individual responsibilities and decision-making authority.

4. Why is there a lack of clarity on responsibilities and decision-making authority?

- Answer: The contract review process lacks defined roles and responsibilities.

5. Why does the contract review process lack defined roles and responsibilities?

- Answer: There is no standardized procedure or documentation outlining the roles and responsibilities of each stakeholder.

Aha! By asking "Why" multiple times, we have identified that the lack of defined roles and responsibilities in the contract review process is one of the root causes of delays. This realization helps us understand that addressing this issue can contribute to improving contract timelines.

A picture is worth a thousand words! Let's analyze the same problem visually. So, in order to visually represent this analysis, let us try to create a fishbone diagram (cause-and-effect diagram) with "Contract Delays" as the problem statement at the head of the fishbone. We could then draw branches for potential causes, such as "Multiple Stakeholders," "Lack of Clarity on Responsibilities," and "No Standardized Procedure." Each cause can be further explored and validated through discussions and data analysis.

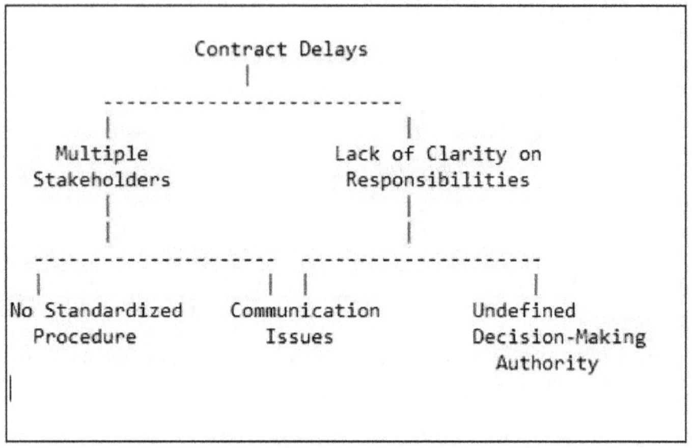

Fish Bone Diagram

This visual can help us develop solutions to address the identified causes, such as creating clear role definitions, establishing a standardized review procedure, or improving communication channels between stakeholders.

Comparative Analysis

Comparative analysis is a valuable technique in diagnostic analytics that involves comparing data sets, performance metrics, or benchmarks to identify patterns, trends, or deviations. It is simply about comparing different sets of data to help us gain insights into the underlying causes of specific outcomes and understand how they measure up against industry standards or best practices.

Let us continue with the example of contracts management.

Comparative analysis in this case could be variance analysis. This technique involves comparing actual contract performance metrics, such as contract cycle time or cost, with planned or expected values. By simply comparing the variances between the actual and planned values, organizations can identify the factors contributing to the deviations and gain a deeper understanding of the root causes.

Let's say you have set a target of completing contracts within 30 days. Through comparative analysis, just compare the actual contract cycle times of different contracts against this target. You may find that some contracts are consistently taking longer to complete, with an average cycle time of, say, 45 days. Now you could concentrate on this subset of contracts. By conducting further analysis, you discover that these delays are primarily occurring when contracts involve complex legal reviews or multiple revisions. With this insight, the organization can delve deeper into the root causes. They can investigate why complex legal reviews are causing delays and explore potential solutions, such as streamlining the review process or involving legal experts earlier in the contract drafting phase. By addressing these underlying issues, they can work towards reducing contract cycle times and improving overall efficiency.

Another technique in comparative analysis is trend analysis. This involves analyzing data over time to identify patterns or trends. In the context of contracts management, trend analysis can help uncover long-term performance trends, such as changes in contract approval times, the frequency of contract amendments, or variations in contract values. By observing these trends, organizations can gain insights into the factors influencing contract performance and make informed decisions to drive improvements.

Benchmarking is yet another powerful comparative analysis technique. It involves comparing organizational performance metrics with industry benchmarks or best practices. In the context of contracts management, organizations can benchmark their contract cycle times, cost savings achieved, or contract compliance rates against industry standards or leading organizations in the same sector. This comparison can highlight areas where the organization is performing well or lagging behind, enabling them to identify opportunities for improvement or learn from best practices to enhance their own contract management processes.

Correlation Analysis

Statistical techniques such as correlation analysis models play a crucial role in diagnostic analytics by helping us identify relationships and dependencies between variables.

What is correlation analysis?

Correlation analysis is a statistical method used to measure the strength and direction of the relationship between two or more variables. It aims to determine whether and how much two variables are related to each other. The result of a correlation analysis is represented by a correlation coefficient, which quantifies the degree of association between the variables.

The correlation coefficient is typically denoted by the symbol "r" and can range from -1 to +1:

- If the correlation coefficient is +1, it indicates a perfect positive correlation, meaning that as one variable increases, the other variable also increases proportionally.

- If the correlation coefficient is -1, it represents a perfect negative correlation, indicating that as one variable increases, the other variable decreases proportionally.
- If the correlation coefficient is close to 0, it suggests a weak or no correlation, meaning that the variables are not significantly related to each other.

Let's consider an example of correlation analysis in the context of procurement in a manufacturing company. Suppose you want to investigate whether there is a relationship between the number of units of a particular raw material purchased and the production output of the company.

Data collection: Over a certain period, you collect data on the number of units of the raw material purchased each month and the corresponding production output of finished products in the same months.

Hypothesis: You want to test the hypothesis that there is a correlation between the quantity of raw material purchased and the production output. The null hypothesis (H0) would be that there is no correlation, while the alternative hypothesis (Ha) would be that there is a correlation.

Statistical analysis: You can perform a correlation analysis using methods like Pearson correlation coefficient or Spearman rank correlation coefficient, depending on the nature of your data (i.e., whether it is continuous or ranked). For simplicity, let's assume you use the Pearson correlation coefficient, denoted by "r."

Interpretation of results: After conducting the correlation analysis, you find that the correlation coefficient "r" is +0.85.

Conclusion: The positive correlation coefficient (+0.85) suggests a strong positive correlation between the quantity of raw material purchased and the production output of finished products. In other words, as the company purchases more units of the raw material, there is a significant increase in the production output.

Implications: This correlation analysis can have several implications for procurement and production planning:

1. Better Inventory Management: The procurement team can use this information to optimize inventory levels of the raw material, ensuring that there are enough units to support increased production needs without excessive stockpiling.
2. Demand Forecasting: By understanding the correlation between raw material purchase and production output, the procurement team can work closely with production planners to forecast demand accurately and procure the necessary materials accordingly.
3. Cost Efficiency: With the knowledge of the correlation, the company can negotiate better pricing and contracts with suppliers based on the projected demand, potentially achieving cost savings.
4. Risk Mitigation: The procurement team can identify potential supply chain risks by monitoring how changes in raw material supply impact production output. This awareness can lead to contingency planning to avoid disruptions.

It's important to remember that correlation does not imply causation. In this example, while there is a strong positive correlation between raw material purchase and production output, other factors may also influence production levels, such as changes in market demand, production technology, or labor availability. Therefore, it is crucial to interpret the results of correlation analysis carefully and consider other variables and potential confounding factors in your analysis.

Let's talk about the contracts management scenario where we want to understand the relationship between contract value and contract duration. We gather data on various contracts, including their respective values and the time it took to complete them. By performing correlation analysis, we can determine the degree to which these two variables are related. A positive correlation would indicate that as the contract value increases, the contract duration also tends to increase. On the other hand, a negative correlation would suggest an inverse relationship, where higher contract values are associated with shorter contract durations. If we find a strong positive correlation between contract value and duration, it suggests that higher-value contracts tend to take longer to complete, possibly due to more extensive negotiations or increased complexity. Now, this can help manage their contracts more effectively by considering factors such as resource allocation, timelines, and risk mitigation strategies.

Regression Analysis

Correlation is a technique where you can compare two variables. However, in a real-world scenario, we often have multiple variables influencing one another. This is where regression analysis can be helpful. Regression is a process of fitting a line based on the data points, particularly in a 2D scenario where one variable is dependent on another.

Let's consider an example: the turnover time of the full contract process is dependent on the turnover process of the legal reviews of the contracts.

Contract Legal Review Time (days)	Full Contract Turnover Time (days)
10	35
8	30
12	38
9	32
15	42
7	28
11	36
13	40
6	25
14	41

Sample Data on Contracts TAT

Let's plot the data points now!

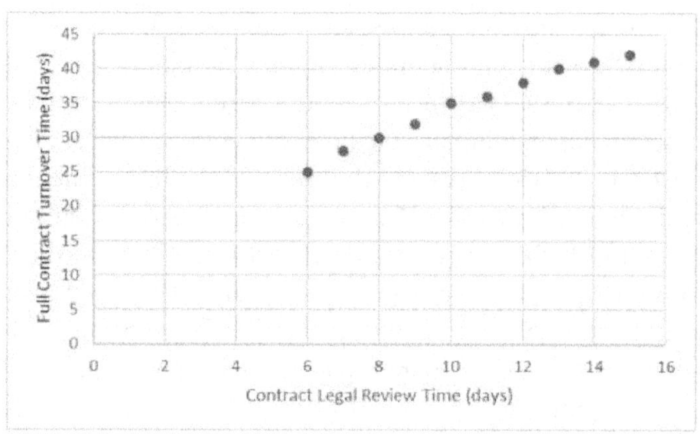

Scatter Plot of Contracts Data

Now, fitting a line to this is what is regression. Let us fit a line now.

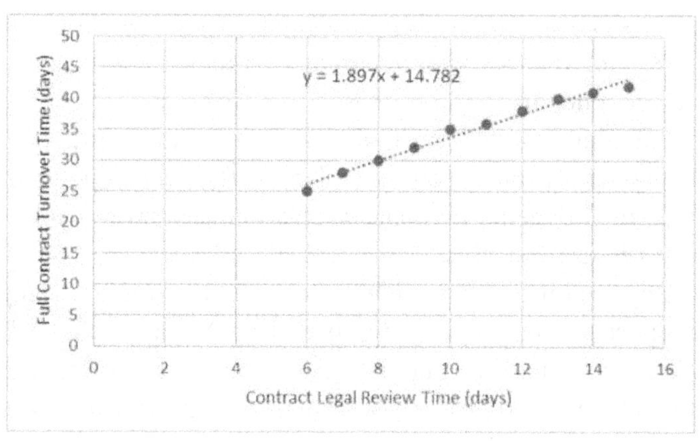

Regression Line for SampleContracts Data

In this scenario, we can approximately fit a line that passes through the maximum number of points, and this is what regression is in its simplest terms. Since we have only one dependent variable here, the equation we get is y = m1*x1 + c (m represents the slope of the line while c is the intercept it makes). You may recall this from what you learned in high school. However, real-world scenarios are not limited to just one dependent variable. We could have multiple variables affecting our 'y.' A regression analysis helps us fit a curve for multiple variables. For example, if we have four dependent variables, the equation will look like this:

$$y = m1*x1 + m2*x2 + m3*x3 + m4*x4 + c$$

Regression analysis is a statistical method used to examine the relationship between one or more independent variables (x - also called predictor variables) and a dependent variable (y - also called the outcome or response variable). Unlike correlation analysis, which focuses on the relationship between two or more variables, regression analysis aims to predict or model the value of the dependent variable based on the values of the independent variables. It allows us to understand how changes in the independent variables affect the dependent variable and helps us make predictions or draw insights from the data.

Regression analysis can be a powerful tool for analyzing complex relationships between multiple variables in real-world scenarios. By understanding the relationships and dependencies among variables, organizations can make informed decisions, forecast outcomes, and optimize processes for better performance.

Clustering

Clustering analysis, as the name clearly specifies, can help us group similar groups based on various attributes. Attributes could be anything based on what you want to group. Let's say - you want to group a collection of contracts.

By applying clustering algorithms like k- means to our contracts dataset, we can identify distinct clusters or segments of contracts with similar characteristics. For example, we may discover a cluster of contracts that have a high probability of early termination due to specific factors such as limited scope or poor performance. This insight allows organizations to proactively address issues and improve contract outcomes within that cluster. Let us see a sample data and understand this.

Contract ID	Contract Term (Months)	Contract Value ($)	Scope	Performance Score	Cluster
1	12	5000	Limited	3.8	Cluster 1
2	6	3000	Comprehensive	4.2	Cluster 2
3	24	8000	Limited	2.5	Cluster 1
4	12	6000	Comprehensive	4.5	Cluster 2
5	18	7000	Comprehensive	3.9	Cluster 2
6	24	9000	Limited	2.1	Cluster 1
7	12	4000	Limited	3.5	Cluster 1
8	18	5500	Comprehensive	4	Cluster 2
9	6	2000	Comprehensive	4.3	Cluster 2
10	24	10000	Limited	2.8	Cluster 1

Clustering on Contracts Data

In this dataset, we have the contract ID, contract term in months, contract value in dollars, scope of the contract (limited or comprehensive), and the performance score. By applying clustering algorithms to this dataset, we can group similar contracts based on these attributes. For example, clustering analysis may reveal two distinct clusters: one cluster with contracts having a limited scope and lower performance scores, and another cluster with contracts having a comprehensive scope and higher performance scores. This insight allows organizations to identify specific contract segments that require attention or improvement. For instance, they can focus on addressing issues related to contracts with limited scope and lower performance scores, implementing corrective actions, and ensuring better outcomes for similar contracts in the future. Popular machine learning algorithms like k-means clustering can be effectively used in such scenarios.

Decision Trees

Using decision tree analysis in contracts management, we can examine a dataset containing information on contract negotiations, stakeholder communication, and contract outcomes. By applying decision tree algorithms, we can construct a decision tree that visually represents the hierarchy of decision rules and identifies the most influential factors in contract success or failure.

A decision tree analysis may reveal that contracts with shorter negotiation periods (less than 30 days) and frequent stakeholder communication (more than three interactions) have a higher likelihood of successful completion. This insight indicates that these variables significantly impact the overall outcome of a contract. By understanding the importance of these factors, organizations can prioritize efficient negotiation processes and foster effective stakeholder engagement to increase the chances of successful contract outcomes.

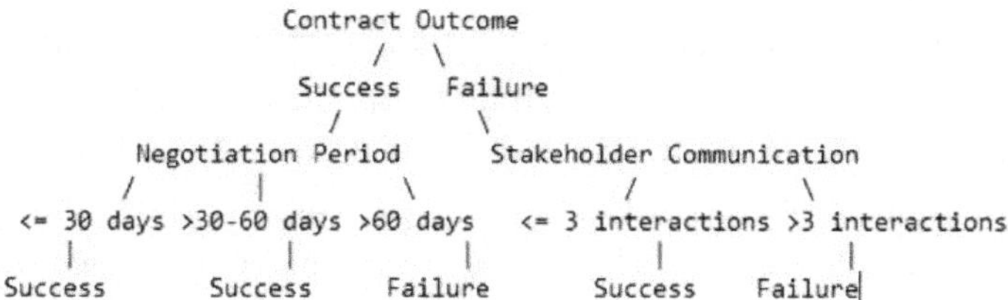

Decision Tree to Analyse Contracts Delay

The decision tree provides a clear and intuitive representation of the decision rules and their impact on contract results. It enables organizations to identify actionable insights and make informed decisions to optimize contract management strategies. By leveraging the specific findings from the decision tree analysis, organizations can proactively focus their efforts on the key variables that drive contract success, leading to improved contract outcomes and stronger relationships with stakeholders. Decision tree analysis is a valuable tool in diagnostic analytics, helping organizations gain a deeper understanding of the factors influencing contract outcomes and guiding them to take targeted actions for better contract management and performance.

Identifying Patterns

Identifying patterns and anomalies involves examining data to uncover trends, relationships, and irregularities. In the context of procurement spend, this technique can help identify patterns of spending behavior, detect anomalies or outliers, and provide valuable insights into procurement performance.

Trend Analysis: Conduct trend analysis to identify patterns or trends in procurement spend over time. This can be done by plotting the spend data on a line chart or conducting time series analysis. By examining the trends, you can identify any significant increases or decreases in spending, seasonal patterns, or overall expenditure patterns. For example, you may notice a consistent increase in spending during certain months of the year, indicating a seasonal trend or a specific event that drives procurement activity.

Anomalies Detection

Employ techniques for anomaly detection to identify any irregular or unusual spending patterns that deviate significantly from the norm. This can involve statistical methods such as outlier analysis, clustering techniques, or machine learning algorithms.

Outlier analysis can help identify transactions with abnormally high or low costs compared to the average spend. These outliers may indicate potential errors, fraudulent activities, or exceptional procurement events that require further investigation.

Machine learning techniques come into play when dealing with complex scenarios where multiple dimensions need to be considered. For instance, combining sourcing data and contracts data with spend data may not be effectively analyzed using simple filters. Machine learning algorithms, such as isolation forests, can handle such scenarios and help identify anomalies that may not be apparent when analyzing data in individual dimensions. The combination of variables from different dimensions can cause anomalies in the overall spend, and machine learning algorithms excel at detecting these complex relationships.

Unveiling Key Performance Indicators

In order to harness the power of diagnostic analytics in procurement, it is essential to identify and utilize key metrics and Key Performance Indicators (KPIs) that provide meaningful insights. We have already seen in chapter 2 that these metrics serve as our compass, guiding us towards making data-driven decisions and improving our procurement practices.

In the previous chapter, we have defined and understood what KPIs mean with a few examples. Now, let's explore some of the most crucial metrics that play a pivotal role in diagnostic analytics. Here, let us walk through a few examples. These metrics have been carefully selected to align with the objectives of procurement processes and provide us with a comprehensive understanding of our performance. However, remember that this list is not exhaustive. Organizations need to think and create a list based on their respective objectives. My attempt here is not to list all the KPIs but rather to give the reader a feel of the diagnostic KPIs.

Supplier Performance Metrics

Supplier Performance Metrics enable us to evaluate supplier performance across various parameters. These metrics include delivery time, quality of goods or services, responsiveness, and adherence to contractual terms. By monitoring and analyzing supplier performance, we can identify areas for improvement, address potential issues, and foster stronger relationships with our suppliers.

A few of the key supplier performance metrics that we utilize could include:

- On-time delivery rate: Measures the percentage of orders delivered by suppliers on time.
- Order accuracy: Reflects the percentage of orders fulfilled without errors or discrepancies.
- Defect rate: Indicates the number of defective products or components received from suppliers.
- Supplier responsiveness: Evaluates how quickly suppliers respond to inquiries or issues.

Analyzing these supplier performance metrics, we can identify underperforming suppliers, pinpoint areas for improvement, and mitigate potential risks within our supply chain. This data-driven approach empowers us to make informed decisions, optimize supplier relationships, and drive continuous improvement in our procurement processes.

Cost Analysis Metrics

Cost analysis metrics are instrumental in diagnostic analytics as they enable us to analyze spending patterns, identify cost-saving opportunities, and evaluate the overall cost-effectiveness of our procurement activities. By delving into cost analysis, we can uncover inefficiencies, negotiate better pricing, and drive significant cost reductions within our organization.

The key cost analysis metrics that we could include:

- Total cost of ownership (TCO): Calculates the total cost associated with acquiring and maintaining a product or service, including direct and indirect costs.
- Cost variance: Compares the actual cost of goods or services with the expected or budgeted cost.
- Cost avoidance: Measures the savings achieved by avoiding unnecessary costs or negotiating better terms with suppliers.
- Cost breakdown by category: Analyzes the distribution of costs across different procurement categories.

Quality Assessment Metrics

Quality assessment metrics are vital for evaluating the quality of goods or services provided by our suppliers. These metrics help us ensure that we receive products or services that meet our expectations and adhere to our quality standards. By tracking and analyzing these metrics, we can identify areas for improvement, address quality issues, and enhance overall supplier performance.

Key quality assessment metrics include:

- efect rate: Measures the number or percentage of defective products or components received from suppliers.
- Customer satisfaction scores: Captures feedback from customers regarding their satisfaction with the quality

of products or services.
- Compliance with quality standards: Evaluates the extent to which suppliers meet established quality standards, industry regulations, or certifications.

Risk Management Metrics

Risk management metrics play a pivotal role in diagnostic analytics by enabling us to assess and mitigate risks associated with our procurement activities. By monitoring and analyzing these metrics, such as supplier reliability, financial stability, and regulatory compliance, we can proactively identify and address potential risks, safeguard our supply chain, and minimize disruptions.

Key risk management metrics include:

- Supplier performance scorecards: Evaluate suppliers based on various performance indicators, including quality, delivery, and compliance.
- Compliance metrics: Measure adherence to regulatory requirements, industry standards, and internal policies.
- Supplier diversity metrics: Assess the extent to which we engage and support diverse suppliers.

These metrics help us in identifying potential risks in our procurement processes, ensuring compliance, and protecting our organization from financial, operational, or reputational risks.

Contract Management Metrics

We have already seen many unstaces where contract management is utmost important. Contract management metrics are essential for evaluating the performance of our contracts, ensuring compliance, and effectively managing the contract lifecycle. By analyzing these metrics, we can optimize contract performance, improve processes, and mitigate risks associated with contract management.

Key contract management metrics include:

- Contract compliance rate: Measures the extent to which parties adhere to the terms and conditions outlined in the contracts.
- Contract cycle time: Measures the time taken to complete the entire contract lifecycle, from negotiation to execution.
- Contract milestone achievement: Tracks the completion of key milestones or deliverables outlined in the contracts.

From Hurdles to Success: Challenges and Best Practices

Doing is not as easy as said, right? We would face challenges here too. For diagnostic analytics, there are various challenges that organizations may encounter. It is important to be aware of these challenges and adopt best practices to overcome them effectively. In this section, we will discuss some common challenges and recommended best practices for the successful implementation of diagnostic analytics. Well, the challenges start right from collecting the data, but we have seen all those in Part 1. Let us now look at the challenges that are specific to advanced analytics.

Challenges

The challenge of resource and skill constraints pertains to the limitations organizations face in terms of the necessary resources, such as budget, technology, and personnel, as well as the skills and expertise required for effective diagnostic analytics. Limited resources may hinder organizations from acquiring advanced analytics tools. Skill constraints refer to the lack of trained professionals with expertise in statistical analysis and data interpretation. To address this challenge, organizations need to allocate sufficient resources for technology and talent acquisition. This may involve training existing employees, hiring skilled technology professionals, or collaborating with external consultants or service providers to bridge skill gaps and ensure the availability of necessary resources for diagnostic analytics initiatives.

Change Management

Change management refers to the challenge of driving organizational and cultural changes to adopt diagnostic analytics practices effectively. This challenge involves overcoming resistance to change, ensuring buy-in from key stakeholders, and aligning organizational goals and processes with the adoption of analytics-driven decision-making. Change management requires strong leadership support, effective communication strategies, and a well-defined roadmap for implementing diagnostic analytics initiatives. It also involves providing training and support to employees to familiarize them with new tools, techniques, and processes. Successful change management facilitates the integration of diagnostic analytics into the organization's procurement practices and ensures its sustained impact and effectiveness.

Best Practices

Advanced Analytics Tools and Platforms

Investing in advanced analytics tools and platforms can simplify the data analysis process and enable organizations to leverage a wide range of statistical techniques. Tools such as R, Python, or specialized analytics software provide capabilities for data exploration, visualization, and modeling, making the analysis more efficient and effective.

Collaboration and Cross-Functional Teams

Building cross-functional teams that include data scientists, analysts, and subject matter experts from procurement and other relevant departments can enhance the effectiveness of diagnostic analytics. Collaboration and knowledge-sharing across teams facilitate a comprehensive understanding of the data and the business context.

Continuous Learning and Skill Development

Organizations should prioritize the development of analytical skills among their employees. Providing training and professional development opportunities in areas such as data analysis, statistical modeling, and data visualization can empower employees to effectively utilize diagnostic analytics techniques and tools.

CHAPTER XIII

Designing your Initial Dashboard

We have already seen in chapter 9, how important is data visualization in the journey of digital transformation. You very well know that a well-designed dashboard serves as a powerful tool for visualizing and monitoring key performance indicators (KPIs), tracking progress towards procurement goals, and facilitating data-driven decision-making. This chapter focuses on the process of designing your initial procurement dashboard, starting from defining objectives and selecting relevant metrics to creating a visually appealing and user-friendly interface.

In this chapter, let us explore the realm of diagnostic analytics in procurement. We will delve into the key principles, methodologies, and best practices that empower procurement professionals to transform raw data into actionable insights. From defining clear objectives for procurement dashboards to crafting compelling data stories, we will uncover how storytelling and visualizations can breathe life into the data, engaging stakeholders and fostering informed decision-making.

Through the lens of procurement analytics, we will address various challenges organizations may encounter in implementing diagnostic analytics and share recommended best practices to overcome them effectively. By understanding the significance of simplicity, clarity, and visual hierarchy, we lay the foundation for a seamless and engaging dashboard design.

This chapter also walks you through the importance of charting a course for dashboard success by aligning analytics efforts with the broader organizational goals. We will explore the impact of transforming data into compelling narratives, giving life to data visualizations, and building a seamless data journey to guide stakeholders through the procurement dashboard's story.

Charting a Course for Dashboard Success

Clearly defining the objectives of the procurement dashboard is utmost important. It serves as a guiding light, helping us align analytics efforts with the broader goals of the organization and enabling effective decision-making processes.

When it comes to procurement analytics, the dashboard is not just a collection of charts and graphs; it is a strategic tool that should reflect the organization's procurement goals and priorities. The primary goal of our dashboard is to empower the end user with a comprehensive view of our procurement landscape, enabling them to identify trends, uncover opportunities, and address challenges effectively. So, it is important that we understand who the end users are. In a given organizational setup, the end users could range from the leadership teams to all the employees in the procurement department who negotiate.

By leveraging data-driven analytics, we should aim to enhance our procurement strategies, optimize supplier relationships, and drive cost savings. Defining clear objectives for the dashboard ensures that it becomes a powerful resource for monitoring performance, identifying areas of improvement, and supporting data-driven decision-making.

What could be the objectives that we could set up for procurement before we build our dashboard? Let me list a few of them here!

- Enhance Visibility: The procurement dashboard should aim to provide clear visibility into procurement activities, including spend analysis, supplier performance, and contract management. It enables stakeholders to access real-time data and gain a comprehensive overview of procurement operations.
- Improve Decision-making: The dashboard helps facilitate informed decision-making by presenting key metrics, performance indicators, and trends. It provides stakeholders with actionable insights to identify cost-saving opportunities, optimize supplier relationships, and mitigate risks.
- Monitor Performance: The dashboard enables the monitoring and tracking of procurement performance against predefined goals and targets. It allows stakeholders to assess the effectiveness of procurement strategies, identify areas for improvement, and measure progress over time.
- Identify Cost Savings: A primary objective of the procurement dashboard is to identify cost-saving opportunities. It helps stakeholders analyze spending patterns, identify areas of excessive spending, and negotiate better terms with suppliers. The dashboard provides visibility into cost-saving initiatives and tracks the actual cost savings achieved.
- Ensure Compliance: The dashboard supports compliance management by monitoring adherence to procurement policies, regulations, and contract terms. It helps identify any non-compliant activities and enables stakeholders to take corrective actions to ensure compliance throughout the procurement process.

- Enhance Supplier Performance: The dashboard facilitates supplier performance management by providing insights into supplier metrics, such as on-time delivery, quality, and responsiveness. It helps identify top-performing suppliers, monitor their performance, and foster productive relationships to drive supplier optimization.
- Streamline Processes: One objective of the procurement dashboard is to streamline procurement processes and improve operational efficiency. It enables stakeholders to identify bottlenecks, streamline workflows, and automate repetitive tasks. The dashboard can highlight areas where process improvements can be made, leading to increased efficiency and reduced cycle times.
- Foster Data-Driven Culture: The procurement dashboard promotes a data-driven culture within the organization. It encourages stakeholders to rely on data and analytics for decision-making, fosters a deeper understanding of procurement trends, and promotes transparency and accountability across the procurement function.

Dashboard Design Principles

When designing a procurement dashboard or, for that matter, any dashboard, simplicity and clarity are fundamental principles that I adhere to. A clean and uncluttered design is crucial in ensuring that users can easily understand and interpret the information presented. We need to create a dashboard that promotes intuitive navigation and minimizes visual distractions.

- Simplicity - To achieve simplicity, I would suggest focusing on presenting the key metrics and insights in a concise and straightforward manner. Avoid overcrowding the dashboard with excessive data or unnecessary visuals that may confuse or overwhelm users. Instead, carefully select the most relevant metrics and display them prominently, allowing users to quickly grasp the essential information.
- Clear Labeling - Clear labels and intuitive navigation are essential elements in ensuring the usability of the dashboard. Each component, whether it is a chart, graph, or table, should be accompanied by clear labels that describe the information being presented. This helps users understand the context and purpose of each visual element, enabling them to make informed decisions based on the data.
- Arrangement of Elements - Furthermore, I pay close attention to the layout and organization of the dashboard. Arranging the elements in a logical order and ensuring that related information is grouped together is key. This helps users navigate through the dashboard effortlessly, finding the specific metrics or insights they are looking for without any confusion.
- No Visual Distractions - Minimizing visual distractions is another key aspect of simplicity and clarity. Avoid unnecessary embellishments or decorative elements that do not contribute to the understanding of the data. By keeping the design clean and focused, users can concentrate on the metrics and insights without any distractions, enabling them to derive meaningful conclusions and take decisive actions. Here's a prototype of an initial procurement dashboard that incorporates the principles of simplicity and clarity.

- Visual Hierarchy - Visual hierarchy in a procurement dashboard is like a well-orchestrated symphony, where each instrument plays its part to guide the listeners' attention and evoke emotions. Just as a conductor leads the orchestra, as a procurement professional, we need to understand the significance of establishing a clear visual hierarchy to direct users' focus and enhance their understanding of the data.

  Imagine the dashboard as a musical score, with each element representing a different instrument or note. The size of the elements acts as the volume of the instruments, allowing us to emphasize important metrics or visuals, like a crescendo building up to a climactic moment. For critical information, I use vibrant and contrasting colors, just like the striking notes of a trumpet or the deep resonance of a cello, capturing the users' attention and creating a memorable impact.

  The placement of elements is akin to the positioning of musicians on a stage. I strategically position key metrics and visuals in prominent areas, such as the conductor's podium, ensuring they take center stage. Supporting information, like the harmonies provided by accompanying instruments, finds its place in less prominent areas, providing context without overpowering the main melody.

  Typography becomes the lyrics of the music, with different font sizes, styles, and weights guiding users' reading flow. Headings and titles take the role of powerful vocals, commanding attention, while supporting text acts as harmonious backing vocals, providing additional details and insights. Bold or italicized text serves as the highlights or key phrases, just as certain words in a song are emphasized for emphasis and emotional impact.

Lastly, grouping and spacing of elements resemble the rhythmic patterns and pauses in a musical composition. I arrange related information into logical groups, using clear headings as the beats that tie them together. Ample spacing between elements creates a harmonious balance, allowing users to read the "musical score" effortlessly and appreciate the individual notes that form the complete melody.

- Crafting Compelling Data Stories - Headlines and captions play a crucial role in capturing users' attention and guiding them through the procurement dashboard's narrative. By using impactful and concise language, these elements highlight key insights, trends, and anomalies in the data. They act as signposts, directing users' focus to significant information and ensuring they grasp the most important takeaways.

  Headlines provide a high-level summary or introduction to a section or visualization, while captions offer context and explanations for specific data points or visualizations. With carefully crafted headlines and captions, users can quickly grasp the essence of the data presented and understand its relevance to their decision-making process. These elements serve as navigational aids, allowing users to follow the storyline and delve deeper into the insights provided by the dashboard. By leveraging clear and compelling headlines and captions, stakeholders can effectively engage with the data, comprehend its implications, and make informed decisions based on the procurement dashboard's narrative.
- Unlocking the Meaning behind the Data - Annotations are a powerful tool to enrich the storytelling experience

within the procurement dashboard. They allow us to provide additional context, explanations, and insights that enhance users‘ understanding of the data. By strategically placing annotations alongside relevant visual elements or data points, we can highlight important details, correlations, or patterns that might otherwise go unnoticed.

For example, suppose we observe a sudden spike in supplier costs during a particular time period. By adding an annotation, we can explain that this increase is due to external factors, such as inflation or changes in market conditions. This contextual information helps stakeholders grasp the underlying reasons behind the data and enables them to make more informed interpretations.

Annotations can also be used to highlight significant events or milestones. For instance, if a supplier achieves a quality rating above a predefined threshold, we can annotate the corresponding data point to recognize this achievement and acknowledge their commitment to excellence. Furthermore, annotations can be used to provide guidance or actionable insights. For instance, if a supplier consistently underperforms in on-time delivery, we can add an annotation suggesting the need for closer monitoring, potential supplier development initiatives, or exploring alternative sourcing options.

Storytelling in Dashboard Design

While data visualization and analytics provide valuable information, the true power lies in the ability to transform data into compelling narratives. Storytelling adds context, emotion, and engagement to the procurement dashboard, enabling stakeholders to understand the insights and take meaningful actions based on them. Let us explore how storytelling can enhance the effectiveness of dashboard design and drive impactful decision-making.

In many conversations with stakeholders, I have come to realize the power of storytelling in dashboard design. It goes beyond simply presenting data and charts; it adds depth, context, and emotion to the insights we want to communicate. Storytelling allows us to engage stakeholders on a deeper level, helping them connect with the data and understand its significance in our procurement efforts. When designing a procurement dashboard, I understand the importance of developing a purposeful narrative. It is essential to align the narrative with our procurement goals and objectives. Whether we aim to identify cost-saving opportunities, address supplier performance gaps, or showcase category insights, a well-crafted narrative helps us convey the story behind the data.

But how do we tell a story?

- Putting Faces to Data

Introducing characters and setting the scene in our dashboard narrative can greatly enhance stakeholder engagement. By giving life to different suppliers and establishing the procurement landscape as the backdrop, we make the data relatable and relevant. Stakeholders can connect with the challenges and opportunities presented in the data, fostering a deeper understanding of the procurement landscape. Let's imagine a procurement dashboard focused on supplier performance in the electronics category. In this narrative-driven dashboard, we can introduce characters representing different suppliers, each with their own unique traits and strengths.

Meet Supplier A, a well-established electronics manufacturer known for their high-quality products and competitive pricing. We can present Supplier A as a reliable and trustworthy partner in the procurement landscape. On the other hand, let's introduce Supplier B, a relatively new player in the market known for their innovative designs and cutting-edge technology. While their prices may be slightly higher, their products offer unique features and differentiation.

By setting the scene as a dynamic and competitive electronics market, we create a relatable context for stakeholders. They can understand the challenges and opportunities in sourcing electronic products and how different suppliers fit into the landscape. Now, let's dive into the data. We can present key performance indicators (KPIs) such as **on-time delivery**, **product quality**, and **pricing competitiveness** for both Supplier A and Supplier B. Using visual representations such as charts, graphs, and icons, we showcase their performance in each category. Through the narrative, we can highlight the strengths and weaknesses of each supplier. For example, Supplier A consistently demonstrates excellent on-time delivery and product quality, making them a reliable choice for timely and high-quality electronics. However, their pricing may be slightly higher compared to other suppliers. On the other hand, Supplier B excels in product innovation and cutting-edge technology, offering unique features that can give our organization a competitive edge. While their prices may be slightly higher, the added value they provide may be worth the investment. By presenting the data in the context of the supplier characters we introduced, stakeholders can connect with the challenges and opportunities represented.

They can see the trade-offs between factors such as price, quality, and innovation, and make more informed decisions based on the narrative we have constructed.

- Transforming Data into Engaging Narratives

This plays a crucial role in our storytelling approach. Identifying conflicts or challenges represented in the data allows us to present the data in a way that reveals these issues. By highlighting fluctuating supplier prices, delivery delays, or quality concerns, we create a sense of urgency and the need for action. The data becomes more than just numbers; it becomes a call to address these challenges and find resolutions.

Let's continue with our example of the procurement dashboard focusing on supplier performance in the electronics category. In this case, we can identify a conflict related to delivery delays that require resolution.

Suppose that in the data analysis, we observe a recurring issue of delivery delays from Supplier B. Their products may have excellent quality and innovative features, but there is a consistent pattern of late deliveries, which can negatively impact our operations and customer satisfaction. To present this conflict and resolution in the storytelling approach, we can create a section in the dashboard dedicated to highlighting the delivery performance of suppliers. Using visual elements such as line charts or bar graphs, we can depict the on-time delivery rate for each supplier over time. In the narrative, we can explain how delivery delays from Supplier B have been causing disruptions in our supply chain, leading to missed production deadlines and dissatisfied customers.

By presenting this challenge in a compelling way, stakeholders can understand the impact of the issue on our organization's overall performance and reputation and take necessary action for resolution.

Now, we shift the focus to the resolution. We can showcase the actions taken to address the delivery delays, such as working closely with Supplier B to identify the root causes and implement corrective measures. We can include data points that reflect improvements in their delivery performance over time, demonstrating the effectiveness of our efforts.

By presenting the conflict and resolution in the storytelling approach, stakeholders are not just confronted with the issue of delivery delays, but also with the proactive steps taken to address it. This approach fosters a sense of urgency and the need for action, driving stakeholders to pay closer attention to the data and actively participate in finding solutions. The conflict and resolution approach adds depth and narrative flow to the procurement dashboard. It transforms the data into a compelling story that engages stakeholders, generates buy-in for necessary actions, and encourages collaboration to overcome challenges. Ultimately, this approach leads to more effective decision-making and improved procurement outcomes.

- Adding Life to Data Visualization

This is another key aspect of our dashboard design. We should leverage icons, images, and illustrations that support our narrative and evoke emotions. By carefully selecting color schemes that convey meaning and draw attention to critical insights, we enhance the visual impact and make the storytelling experience more compelling.

Let's discuss this aspect with our example of the procurement dashboard focusing on supplier performance in the electronics category.

To enhance the storytelling experience, we can incorporate icons, images, and illustrations that align with the narrative and evoke emotions. For instance, when discussing the challenges and opportunities presented by different suppliers, we can use icons or images that represent each supplier. These visual representations help stakeholders quickly identify and connect with the suppliers being discussed.

Additionally, we can leverage color schemes to convey meaning and draw attention to critical insights. For example, we can use a color-coding system to indicate supplier performance levels. Green can represent high-performing suppliers, yellow can indicate average performance, and red can signify suppliers with performance issues. By using such color schemes consistently throughout the dashboard, stakeholders can easily identify and interpret supplier performance at a glance.

When presenting data related to cost savings or efficiency improvements, we can use visual metaphors or illustrations that reinforce these concepts. For instance, we can incorporate images of a rising graph or an upward arrow to symbolize cost savings, while images of gears or a well-oiled machine can represent improved efficiency. The sky is the limit to get creative here. These visual cues not only capture stakeholders' attention but also evoke emotions associated with positive outcomes. They make the data more relatable and memorable, contributing to a more engaging and impactful storytelling experience.

- Building a Seamless Data Journey

To guide stakeholders through the narrative, its a good idea to structure our dashboard in a logical and sequential manner. We should be able to present the data in a cohesive flow, allowing stakeholders to follow the story step by step. This sequential presentation builds understanding and leads to meaningful conclusions, empowering stakeholders to make informed decisions based on the narrative we have shared.

As an example, let me walk you through a structure that will help to guide stakeholders through the narrative. Let us ensure a logical flow within the dashboard, presenting data and insights in a sequential manner that builds upon each other. We will organize the sections in a logical order, such as starting with an overview, followed by specific metrics, and concluding with insights and recommendations.

Let us begin now to see what the structure would mean to a dashboard.

- Landing Tab: In the landing section of the procurement dashboard, where we provide an overview of the procurement landscape and the objectives of the analysis, we can include key metrics and KPIs that provide a high-level understanding of supplier performance. The table below shows some typical examples with an additional column indicating the recommended visualization type for each KPI.

Metric	Description	Recommended Visualization
Total Spend	The total amount of procurement spend across all suppliers. Also, the spend of previous year can be shown, to set the comparison.	Number Card
Supplier Count	The number of suppliers currently being evaluated. Also, the spend of previous year can be shown, to set the comparison.	Number Card
Supplier Performance Score	A composite score or rating representing the overall performance of each supplier.	Heatmap or Gauge Chart
On-Time Delivery Rate	The percentage of orders delivered on time by each supplier.	Bar Chart or Line Chart
Quality Index	An index or rating capturing the overall quality performance of suppliers.	Bar Chart or Radar Chart
Supplier Diversity	The representation of suppliers in terms of categories, regions, or minority-owned businesses.	Bar Graph or Treemap

Landing Tab

- Cost Analysis Tab: In the cost analysis section of the procurement dashboard, we focus on operational key performance indicators (KPIs) that provide insights into the cost-related aspects of our procurement activities. These KPIs help us monitor and evaluate the efficiency and effectiveness of our procurement processes, supplier relationships, and cost-saving initiatives. By visualizing these metrics using bar charts or pie charts, we can effectively compare and highlight cost performance across suppliers, categories, and identify areas for improvement. The key cost analysis metrics and the corresponding KPIs that can be included in this section are shown in the table below.

Metric	Description	Recommended Visualization
Spend by Supplier	The total procurement spend allocated to each supplier.	Bar Chart or Pie Chart
Spend by Category	The distribution of procurement spend across different categories.	Bar Chart or Treemap
Cost Savings Achieved	The amount of cost savings generated through procurement initiatives.	Number Card or Line Chart
Strategic Sourcing Percentage	The proportion of procurement spend that is strategically sourced.	Pie Chart or Donut Chart

Cost Analysis Tab

- Quality Assessment Tab: In the quality assessment section of the procurement dashboard, we shift our focus to key performance indicators (KPIs) that provide insights into the quality aspects of our procurement processes and supplier performance. These KPIs help us monitor and evaluate the quality of products or services delivered by our suppliers, identify areas of improvement, and ensure that quality standards are met consistently. By visualizing these metrics using line graphs or stacked bar charts, we can effectively track quality performance over time and compare performance across suppliers.

Metric	Description	Recommended Visualization
Defect Rate	The percentage of defective products or services delivered by suppliers.	Stacked Bar Chart or Line Graph
Customer Complaints	The number of complaints received from customers regarding product quality or service.	Bar Chart or Heatmap
Product Ratings	Ratings or scores given by customers or internal stakeholders for product quality or service satisfaction.	Radar Chart or Bar Chart
On-Time Delivery Performance	The percentage of orders delivered by suppliers within the agreed-upon timeframe.	Line Graph or Bar Chart
Supplier Corrective Action Requests (SCARs)	The number of corrective action requests raised against suppliers due to quality issues.	Number Card or Bullet Chart

Quality Assessment Tab

- Delivery Reliability Tab: Next, focus on delivery reliability metrics such as on-time delivery rates, lead time, or order fulfillment. Present these metrics in a visually engaging manner, such as with gauges or progress bars, to highlight the performance of each supplier.

Metric	Description	Recommended Visualization
On-Time Delivery Rate	The percentage of orders delivered by suppliers within the agreed timeframe.	Gauge Chart or Progress Bar
Lead Time	The time taken from order placement to delivery by each supplier.	Line Chart or Bar Chart
Order Fulfillment Percentage	The percentage of orders fulfilled completely by each supplier.	Stacked Bar Chart or Pie Chart
Delivery Accuracy	The accuracy of deliveries, measured by the percentage of error-free deliveries.	Heatmap or Radar Chart
Backorder Rate	The rate of backordered items due to supplier delivery delays.	Bullet Chart or Number Card

Delivery Reliability Tab

- Conclusion and Recommendations Tab: Summarize the findings from the previous sections and provide key insights and conclusions. Based on the narrative built through the sequential presentation of data, offer recommendations for improvement, such as supplier optimization, contract renegotiation, or quality improvement initiatives.

CHAPTER XIV

Takeaways - Part 2

Now would you agree that procurement analytics is a powerful tool that empowers organizations to optimize procurement processes, enhance supplier relationships, and drive cost savings. Before concluding this part, I would like to quickly walk you through the key take aways from this part of the book.

- Procurement Analytics as a Strategic Driver:

Procurement analytics plays a crucial role in transforming procurement from a transactional function to a strategic driver of organizational success. By leveraging data and analytics, procurement professionals can optimize processes, drive cost savings, and enhance supplier relationships.

- Data Visualization for Effective Communication:

Data visualization techniques and tools are essential for presenting complex data insights in a clear and compelling manner. Using charts, graphs, and dashboards, procurement professionals can make data easily understandable and actionable for stakeholders.

- Identifying Relevant Metrics and KPIs:

Selecting the right metrics and Key Performance Indicators (KPIs) is essential in measuring procurement performance and aligning with organizational goals. These metrics provide valuable insights into spend patterns, supplier performance, and risk management.

- Defining Clear Problem Statements:

Defining clear problem statements is crucial for effective procurement analytics. Understanding the problem, engaging stakeholders, and formulating hypotheses enable procurement professionals to focus on finding actionable insights.

- Diagnostic Analytics Methodologies:

Diagnostic analytics methodologies, such as root cause analysis, comparative analysis, correlation analysis, regression analysis, and data mining, help uncover insights and root causes behind procurement data, leading to opportunities for improvement.

- Overcoming Challenges and Best Practices:

Implementing diagnostic analytics in procurement may face challenges such as resource constraints and change management. Adopting best practices, including investing in advanced analytics tools, fostering collaboration, and continuous skill development, ensures successful implementation.

- Effective Dashboard Design:

Dashboard design principles, such as simplicity, clarity, and visual hierarchy, are vital in presenting procurement data effectively. Incorporating storytelling techniques and visual cues enhances stakeholder engagement and decision-making.

- Transforming Data into Compelling Narratives:

Storytelling in procurement analytics adds context, emotion, and engagement to data insights. By crafting narratives with conflicts, resolutions, and visual elements, stakeholders can connect with the data and take meaningful actions.

AI Innovation

PART 3

"AI, like electricity or the internet, is a tool that will enable us to solve many problems that previously seemed unsolvable."

- Andrew Ng

CHAPTER XV

Introduction to AI in Procurement

We are all aware that AI innovation has revolutionized numerous industries, pushing the boundaries of what was once thought possible. From healthcare to finance, transportation to entertainment, AI has been a catalyst for transformative change. By leveraging advanced algorithms, machine learning techniques, and vast amounts of data, AI has enabled the development of intelligent systems that can learn, reason, and make decisions. This chapter is meant to set the stage for exploring the world of AI innovation in procurement.

The impact of AI innovation is far-reaching. It has the potential to enhance efficiency, accuracy, and productivity across various sectors, including procurement. AI-powered technologies, such as natural language processing, computer vision, and robotics, are enabling us to automate complex tasks, gain valuable insights from data, and create personalized experiences for users. With continuous advancements in AI research and development, we are already experiencing greater breakthroughs that will shape the way we live, work, and interact with technology in the future.

Equipped with knowledge of Data and Analytics in the last two parts, we now zoom in and check the capabilities of AI that can be leveraged in procurement. Since not all my readers would have an AI background, I have dedicated chapter 16 to explain the AI technologies that could be used for typical procurement data. This chapter discusses the techniques and algorithms that could potentially be used for a particular technique. However, I have not gone into explaining the algorithms here. I would suggest you refer to any standard YouTube videos or other available material to delve into the algorithms.

After gaining an understanding of the available techniques, we will be ready to apply them to our procurement data. The next chapter focuses on the development of use cases based on the data. It provides insight into how different sources of data can be combined to define a problem and apply AI to solve it. The chapter primarily emphasizes the multidimensional problem-solving capacity of AI. Please note that this will only aid in the thought process of building AI use cases. Each organization must customize their solutions based on their data, business goals, and available technology.

The use case studies discussed in this chapter are purely derived from my thinking and can generally be relevant to any typical procurement business. However, it is important to remember that one size does not fit all.

Similar to the evolution observed in nature, AI is also evolving. It started with statistics in the early 1800s and evolved into AI in the early 1900s. In the last decade, we have witnessed significant evolution in AI. However, it will not stop here. It is like having your food served on a plate and finding a sauce bottle to add flavor. Initially, you press, and nothing comes out, but eventually, the first drop appears, followed by subsequent drops. Then, there comes a point where the sauce comes out in big lumps. This is where we are currently. We are witnessing major innovations like ChatGPT, which are making AI stronger and stronger. And it is certain that AI will continue to evolve. Therefore, from a procurement perspective, it is important for us to be prepared for what will be a game changer. Chapter 18 is dedicated to exploring the latest trends in AI. I have also taken a step forward to consider how AI could revolutionize procurement in the future and what bold steps we need to take to align procurement business goals with the latest technology.

While the progress of AI innovation may seem positive and promising, we must also consider the flip side of the coin. As AI continues to advance, it becomes essential to address ethical considerations, including privacy, fairness, and accountability. This is crucial to ensure that the benefits of AI are harnessed responsibly and for the greater good of society. The final chapter in this section of the book is dedicated to understanding the ethics of using AI in general, as well as specifically in the context of procurement.

Prepare yourself to embark on a journey of discovery, uncovering the boundless possibilities that AI brings to the procurement industry.

CHAPTER XVI

Key AI Technologies

Let's delve into three key AI technologies that are transforming the procurement landscape: machine learning, natural language processing (NLP), and AI based robotic process automation (RPA).

Machine learning plays a vital role by enabling systems to learn from data and improve performance without explicit programming. It helps in predicting outcomes, making recommendations, and identifying patterns in vast amounts of data.

Natural language processing (NLP) enhances communication and analysis by extracting valuable insights from unstructured data sources, such as text documents, emails, and social media. NLP enables the understanding of human language and facilitates natural language interactions between humans and machines.

Robotic process automation (RPA) automates repetitive and rule-based tasks, enabling faster and more accurate execution of procurement processes. This technology frees up procurement professionals from mundane tasks, allowing them to focus on strategic activities that require human expertise.

In addition to these technologies, Cognitive AI is gaining prominence. It combines multiple AI technologies to simulate human thought processes, generating actionable insights and augmenting procurement intelligence.

Before we delve into the opportunities and possibilities that AI brings to the world of procurement, I will provide an overview of the basic AI methodologies and relevant algorithms. This explanation is especially useful for those who have limited knowledge of AI and its functions.

Machine Learning: Unlocking Intelligent Insights

In a very broad sense, we all know that machine learning is a subset of artificial intelligence that focuses on enabling computer systems to learn from data and improve their performance without explicit programming.

In the realm of procurement, machine learning techniques are utilized to automate processes, analyze vast amounts of data, and make accurate predictions. Let's explore various machine learning techniques commonly applied in procurement, such as supervised learning, unsupervised learning, and reinforcement learning.

We will examine how the aforementioned techniques can be used to automate processes in procurement, such as supplier selection, demand pattern prediction, inventory level optimization, and detection of fraudulent activities.

Supervised Learning

Supervised learning is a machine learning technique where an algorithm learns patterns and relationships from labeled training data to make predictions or decisions. In supervised learning, the training data comprises input features (independent variables or predictors) and corresponding labels (dependent variables or target variables).

Let's consider a scenario where a child, named Emily, is learning the names of fruits using the steps of supervised learning. Emily's parents are eager to assist her in learning about different fruits, so they decide to teach her using supervised learning.

Labeled Training Data: Emily's parents gather a collection of fruits, including apples, oranges, bananas, and grapes. They create labeled cards with pictures of each fruit and write the fruit's name on the back of each card. The pictures represent the input features, while the written names on the cards represent the labels.

Input Features: The pictures of the fruits on the cards serve as the input features. Each card displays a different fruit, providing visual information to Emily.

Target Variable: The written names on the back of the cards represent the target variable or labels. These names represent the desired output that Emily should learn to associate with each fruit picture.

Learning Algorithm: Emily's parents decide to employ a simple learning algorithm to help her understand and remember the names of the fruits. They start by showing Emily one fruit card at a time, displaying the fruit's picture while pronouncing its name aloud. This process enables Emily to establish a connection between the visual input (the picture) and the desired output (the name).

Model Evaluation and Prediction: After repeated exposure to the fruit cards and their names, Emily's parents assess her learning progress. They randomly show her some fruit cards without revealing the names and ask her to identify each fruit by its name. They measure Emily's accuracy in recognizing and correctly labeling the fruits to evaluate how well she has learned.

Over time, Emily's continuous practice and exposure to various fruit cards lead to improvement in her ability to recognize and correctly name the fruits. She develops a mental model that connects the visual features of each fruit with its corresponding name. Through the process of supervised learning, Emily gradually enhances her understanding and vocabulary related to different fruits.

Based on my experience and research with procurement data, I have identified several areas where supervised learning can be applied to automate and enhance decision-making processes. Let me share some examples:

- Supplier Selection: In the supplier selection process, procurement professionals can utilize supervised learning to train models on historical supplier performance data. By labeling suppliers as "good" or "poor" based on criteria such as delivery reliability, quality performance, or customer satisfaction, the model can learn patterns and make predictions regarding the likelihood of a supplier meeting performance criteria. This assists in ranking suppliers and making informed decisions during supplier selection.
- Demand Forecasting: Accurate demand forecasting is crucial for effective procurement planning. Supervised learning can be employed to analyze demand forecasting by utilizing various types of historical data, including purchase order (PO) data, supplier data, and sourcing data. Each of these data sources provides valuable insights that contribute to accurate demand forecasting. By training models on this data, procurement professionals can predict future demand more accurately, enabling them to optimize and plan procurement activities accordingly.
- Pricing Optimization: Determining optimal pricing for products or services is a critical aspect of procurement. Supervised learning can be applied to analyze historical

pricing data, market trends, competitor pricing, and customer behavior. By training models on this data, procurement professionals can make pricing predictions, identify pricing patterns, and optimize pricing strategies to maximize profitability.

- Fraud Detection: Detecting fraudulent activities in procurement transactions is vital for preventing financial losses and maintaining ethical practices. Supervised learning can be utilized to develop fraud detection models by training them on historical transaction data. By labeling transactions as "fraudulent" or "legitimate," the model can learn patterns and identify suspicious activities, enabling procurement professionals to take appropriate actions and mitigate risks.

Unsupervised Learning

Unsupervised learning is a machine learning technique where the algorithm learns from unlabeled data to discover patterns, relationships, or structures within the data.

Let's revisit our example of Emily, the child learning the names of fruits, in the context of unsupervised learning. In unsupervised learning, Emily would explore a set of unlabeled fruits and attempt to identify patterns or similarities among them without any prior knowledge of their names.

Emily begins by examining a basket of fruits that includes apples, oranges, bananas, and grapes. She observes their various shapes, colors, and sizes. She notices that some fruits are round while others are elongated. Additionally, she observes that fruits can have different colors, such as red, orange, yellow, or green. Without knowing the actual names of the fruits, Emily starts grouping them based on these similarities.

Through unsupervised learning, Emily employs clustering algorithms to automatically group similar fruits together based on their characteristics. These algorithms analyze the features of the fruits, such as shape, color, and size, and identify clusters or groups that exhibit similar attributes. This enables Emily to uncover patterns and relationships among the fruits.

During this process, Emily may discover that apples and oranges are often grouped together due to their shared round shapes and the possibility of being red or orange in color. On the other hand, bananas might form a separate cluster because of their elongated shape and yellow color. Grapes, being small and round, might form another distinct cluster.

The key aspect of unsupervised learning is that it doesn't rely on pre-defined labels or categories. Instead, it allows the algorithm to uncover hidden structures or patterns in the data independently. Emily's ability to identify clusters of fruits based on their shared characteristics resembles how unsupervised learning algorithms find clusters or patterns in data without prior knowledge of class labels.

Unsupervised learning is valuable in procurement as well. I am listing a few use cases here to demonstrate how unsupervised learning can enable procurement professionals to gain valuable insights, discover hidden patterns, and make informed decisions:

- Spend Analysis: Unsupervised learning can be used to analyze and categorize spend data from various sources, such as purchase orders, invoices, and contracts. The algorithm can automatically cluster similar transactions based on attributes like product categories, suppliers, and cost. This helps in identifying spending patterns, detecting anomalies, and gaining insights into purchasing behavior, which can inform strategic sourcing decisions, supplier consolidation, and cost-saving initiatives.

- Supplier Segmentation: Unsupervised learning techniques like clustering can be employed to segment suppliers based on their characteristics and performance. The algorithm can analyze supplier attributes such as quality metrics, delivery times, pricing, and responsiveness. By clustering similar suppliers together, procurement professionals can gain a deeper understanding of supplier portfolios, identify strategic supplier groups, and tailor supplier management strategies accordingly.
- Market Basket Analysis: Unsupervised learning can be utilized to uncover associations and relationships between products or services in procurement. By analyzing historical transaction data, the algorithm can identify frequently co-occurring items or services in purchase orders. This helps in understanding cross-selling opportunities, optimizing product bundling, and improving demand planning and inventory management strategies.
- Fraud Detection: When labeled data is not available to detect fraudulent transactions, unsupervised learning can play a crucial role in detecting fraudulent activities in procurement processes. By analyzing data such as purchase orders, invoices, and payment records, the algorithm can identify patterns indicative of fraud or

irregularities. This can help in flagging suspicious transactions, reducing financial risks, and enhancing overall procurement integrity.

- Demand Pattern Recognition: Unsupervised learning techniques like clustering and pattern recognition can be applied to identify and understand demand patterns in procurement. By analyzing historical demand data, the algorithm can automatically group similar demand patterns, uncover seasonality, identify trends, and make predictions. This assists in demand forecasting, inventory optimization, and proactive procurement planning.

Reinforcement Learning

Reinforcement learning is a machine learning technique where an agent learns to make decisions by interacting with an environment and receiving feedback in the form of rewards or penalties. Although it is predominantly used in the gaming industry, there are limited use cases for reinforcement learning in procurement compared to supervised and unsupervised learning. However, let's try to explore the potential opportunities for reinforcement learning in procurement after gaining a deeper understanding of the concept.

Let's continue with the example of Emily to explain reinforcement learning. Emily's objective is to train her robot dog, Buddy, to perform tricks using a reward-based system. Buddy starts with no knowledge of any tricks and relies on Emily's guidance to learn. Emily has a set of tricks in mind that she wants Buddy to learn, such as "sit," "roll over," and "fetch."

Initially, Emily randomly commands Buddy to perform a trick. If Buddy successfully executes the trick, Emily rewards him with a treat and praises him. However, if Buddy fails to perform the requested trick, Emily withholds the treat and provides gentle correction.

Through repeated interactions, Buddy learns to associate specific commands with certain actions. For instance, when Emily says "sit," Buddy learns to associate it with sitting down. As Buddy receives rewards and penalties based on his performance, he gradually enhances his ability to understand and respond to Emily's commands.

Over time, Buddy starts to recognize patterns and generalizes his learning. He understands that "sit" means to sit down in various contexts and locations. Similarly, he associates "roll over" with rolling onto his back and "fetch" with retrieving an object.

Natural Language Processing: Enhancing Communication

Natural Language Processing (NLP) is another critical AI technology that plays a significant role in procurement. NLP focuses on enabling computers to understand, interpret, and generate human language. In this section, we explore how NLP enhances communication, analysis, and decision-making in procurement. Let us see what NLP offers.

Text Classification

Text classification is the process of categorizing text documents into predefined categories. It involves training machine learning models on labeled data to automatically assign categories to new, unseen text data.

Imagine you have a large collection of books in your library, but they are all jumbled up and unorganized. You want to sort them into different categories, such as fiction, non-fiction, mystery, romance, and so on. However, you don't have the time to read each book and manually categorize them. Text classification in natural language processing (NLP) is like having a smart librarian who can automatically categorize the books for you. The librarian is trained using a set of books that are already categorized. They learn the patterns and characteristics of each category by reading the labeled books. For example, they learn that mystery books often involve crimes and suspense, while romance books focus on love stories. Once the librarian has learned from the labeled books, you can give them a new, unseen book and ask which category it belongs to. Using the knowledge they gained from the training, they can quickly analyze the text of the book and assign it to the appropriate category. The process of training the librarian involves exposing them to a large number of labeled books. They learn to recognize patterns, keywords, and other features that are indicative of each category. This way, they can generalize their understanding to correctly classify new, unseen books.

In NLP, the machine learning models are like the smart librarians. They are trained on a dataset of labeled texts, where each text is associated with a specific category. The models learn to identify important features, words, and patterns that distinguish one category from another.

Once the model is trained, it can be used to classify new, unseen texts automatically. For example, you can provide the model with a new article or a customer review, and it will predict which category it belongs to. This can be incredibly useful in various applications, such as organizing documents, filtering spam emails, sentiment analysis of customer feedback, or even identifying fake news.

By automating the categorization process, text classification saves a lot of time and effort. It allows us to quickly analyze large volumes of text data, gain insights, and make informed decisions based on the categorized information. And in procurement we are always equipped with large datasets. Let me list down few use cases in procurement where text classification would make an impact.

- **Supplier Risk Assessment**: By classifying supplier-related information, such as financial statements, news articles, and compliance reports, text classification can assist in assessing the risk associated with different suppliers. This helps in making informed decisions when selecting and managing suppliers.

- **Spend Management**: Text classification in procurement can cluster spend into granular activities by analyzing SOWs or item descriptions. Machine learning models learn from labeled data to assign new spend items to predefined categories. This enables detailed tracking, analysis, and optimization of expenses. By standardizing and automating the classification process, procurement professionals gain better visibility and make data-driven decisions. It streamlines spend analysis, identifies cost-saving opportunities, and improves financial reporting accuracy. Text classification enhances procurement efficiency and drives cost efficiencies in managing spend activities.

- **Compliance Monitoring**: Text classification can be used for compliance monitoring in procurement by analyzing text data such as contracts, policies, and regulations. By training machine learning models on labeled compliance-related documents, the models can automatically classify new documents as compliant or non-compliant based on predefined criteria. This allows procurement professionals to quickly identify potential compliance issues, track adherence to regulations, and take necessary actions. Text classification enhances compliance monitoring by automating the process, reducing manual effort, and ensuring consistent adherence to compliance standards. It helps organizations mitigate risks, maintain regulatory compliance, and uphold ethical business practices in procurement operations.

Text Summarization

Text summarization techniques condense lengthy text documents into shorter summaries, capturing the key points and main ideas. It can be useful for extracting essential information from large volumes of text.

Imagine you have a long, complex document with lots of information that you need to understand quickly. Text summarization is like having a helpful friend who reads the document for you and provides a concise summary, capturing the most important points and key ideas. It's like getting the "cliff notes" version of a book or a movie trailer that gives you a brief overview of the story. Text summarization uses advanced algorithms to analyze the content, identify the main themes, and generate a condensed summary that captures the essence of the text.

This can be incredibly useful in procurement when you need to review multiple documents, contracts, or reports efficiently and get a quick understanding of their content without reading every word. It saves time, allows you to focus on critical information, and helps you make informed decisions based on the summarized content.

Question Answering

Question answering systems aim to automatically generate accurate answers to questions posed in natural language. They can be trained on specific domains or utilize large-scale language models to provide relevant answers.

Imagine you have a personal assistant who can answer any question you ask. Question answering in natural language processing is like having that assistant who understands your questions and provides accurate answers based on a given text or knowledge base. It's like having a conversation with a knowledgeable expert who can provide instant responses. For example, you could ask, "What is the delivery time for Supplier X?" and the system would analyze the available data and provide you with the specific answer. Question answering systems use advanced algorithms to understand the context of the question, search for relevant information, and generate a precise answer. In procurement, this can be invaluable for quickly retrieving specific information from contracts, supplier databases, or other sources, saving time and enabling informed decision-making.

Through some examples and use cases, I will illustrate the practical applications of NLP in procurement in the coming sections. I will showcase how NLP technologies can streamline supplier communication, improve contract management, enhance market intelligence, and facilitate collaboration among procurement teams.

AI based Robotic Process Automation: Streamlining Procurement Operations

Robotic Process Automation (RPA) when combined with AI technology can automate repetitive and rule-based tasks within procurement operations. RPA software, often referred to as "bots," can mimic human interactions with computer systems to perform tasks such as data entry, document processing, and system integration. By automating these mundane and time-consuming activities, RPA enables procurement professionals to focus on more strategic and value-added tasks. By implementing Robotic Process Automation (RPA) in procurement, organizations can reap numerous benefits.

- **enhanced efficiency** - as RPA automates tasks, leading to faster completion times and a reduction in errors. This increased speed and accuracy can significantly improve overall productivity in procurement operations.
- **reduction in manual workload** - RPA takes care of repetitive and rule-based tasks, freeing up procurement professionals to focus on more strategic activities that require their expertise. This allows them to dedicate their time to activities such as supplier relationship management, strategic sourcing, and contract negotiation.
- **promotes standardization and compliance** - The automation of tasks ensures that predefined rules and

protocols are consistently followed, reducing the risk of deviations or non-compliance. This is particularly important in areas such as contract management, where adherence to contractual obligations is critical.

- **provides organizations with scalability and flexibility** - The software robots can handle large volumes of data and tasks, allowing procurement teams to manage increasing workloads without the need for additional human resources. RPA can also be easily adapted and scaled as per changing business needs, enabling organizations to respond quickly to evolving market dynamics.

Now, let's take a look at the Various applications of RPA within procurement.

RPA can be leveraged to automate a wide range of tasks and processes, streamlining procurement operations and driving efficiency. Let us discuss some key applications of RPA in procurement.

- Purchase Order (PO) Creation: RPA bots can automate the creation of purchase orders by extracting relevant information from requisitions or supplier portals, populating the necessary fields, and submitting the orders to suppliers. This eliminates manual data entry and ensures accuracy and timeliness.
- Invoice Processing: RPA can be utilized to automate invoice processing, including data extraction, validation, and matching with purchase orders and receipts. Bots can perform tasks such as invoice scanning, data entry, and reconciliation, reducing the time and effort required for manual processing.

- Supplier Onboarding: RPA bots can streamline the supplier onboarding process by automating tasks such as collecting and verifying supplier information, conducting due diligence checks, and updating supplier databases. This ensures a smooth and efficient onboarding experience while maintaining data accuracy.
- Contract Management: RPA can automate contract management processes, including contract creation, review, and renewal. Bots can extract relevant data from contracts, monitor contract milestones, and send automated notifications for renewals or terminations, ensuring compliance and minimizing the risk of contract-related issues.
- Data Entry and Validation: RPA can automate data entry tasks by extracting data from various sources, such as emails or spreadsheets, and populating the required fields in procurement systems. Bots can also perform data validation and reconciliation to ensure data accuracy and consistency.
- Supplier Performance Tracking: RPA bots can retrieve data from supplier performance metrics, such as delivery times or quality scores, and generate automated reports or dashboards for tracking and analysis. This provides real-time visibility into supplier performance and facilitates data-driven decision-making.
- Spend Analysis: RPA can automate the process of extracting and consolidating spend data from multiple systems or sources, enabling procurement professionals to analyze and identify cost-saving opportunities, negotiate better contracts, and optimize procurement strategies.

While Robotic Process Automation (RPA) offers numerous benefits in procurement, there are also challenges and considerations that organizations need to address during implementation. These challenges include:

- Process Selection: Choosing the right processes for automation is crucial. Not all processes are suitable for RPA, and it's essential to identify tasks that are repetitive, rule-based, and high in volume to maximize the benefits of automation.
- Data Security and Privacy: With the automation of tasks, sensitive procurement data is handled by RPA bots. Organizations must ensure robust security measures to protect data integrity, confidentiality, and privacy throughout the automation process.
- Bot Governance: Managing and governing RPA bots is essential to maintain control and ensure compliance. This includes defining access controls, monitoring bot activities, and establishing protocols for bot management, updates, and version control.
- Workforce Dynamics: The introduction of RPA can impact the dynamics of the procurement workforce. Some tasks previously performed by humans may be automated, requiring reskilling or redeployment of employees. Organizations need to plan for the workforce implications and provide appropriate training and support to employees.

CHAPTER XVII

AI Applications in Procurement

In the previous chapter, we explored the various AI technologies relevant to procurement and their potential use cases. However, it is essential to align these technologies with the specific objectives of an organization to create impactful solutions. In this chapter, we will delve into four different use cases in procurement and discuss the potential impact they can have once implemented. We will also provide a step-by-step process for each use case, guiding organizations on how to successfully implement AI solutions. Let us explore the inner workings, applications, and real-world examples of AI technology. I will showcase how these technologies are leveraged to automate supplier selection, predict demand patterns, streamline procurement operations, enhance contract management to enable proactive decision-making.

Intelligent Sourcing and Supplier Management

In procurement, one of the challenges we face is how to effectively score suppliers based on their past performance using AI techniques. By leveraging advanced algorithms such as clustering or other unsupervised learning approaches, we can analyze the historical data of suppliers. This allows us to identify patterns and similarities among suppliers, enabling us to assign scores based on their performance, quality metrics, delivery times, pricing, and even customer feedback.

Imagine having an AI-powered scoring system that objectively evaluates and ranks suppliers based on their track record. This system helps us make informed decisions during the sourcing process. It provides us with an efficient and consistent way to assess suppliers and select the most suitable ones for our organization's needs.

Let us put this step by step to get an outcome driven solution

Problem:

The problem addressed is the need for efficient and effective supplier selection in procurement. A large organization in general has vast amount of data at its disposal, including supplier performance metrics, historical delivery times, quality ratings, and pricing information. However, manually analyzing this data to identify patterns and determine the most suitable suppliers is time-consuming and prone to human biases. They need a systematic and data-driven approach to select suppliers based on objective criteria.

Data used:

In order to create a holistic scoring model for a supplier, it is important to understand all the data sources that could affect the model. In general, we have three main systems where supplier data is stored in procurement systems – SAP Ariba which stores the meta data of sourcing, transactional data (SAP – SRM) and Supplier Master data. Let's first understand what all data in general would be available in each of these systems.

In the Ariba SAP sourcing system, the metadata columns typically available include:

- Supplier ID: Unique identifier for each supplier.

- Supplier Name: The name or business entity of the supplier.
- Supplier Type: Categorization of the supplier based on predefined types (e.g., manufacturer, distributor, service provider).
- Supplier Location: The geographical location of the supplier, such as country or region.
- Supplier Contact Information: Contact details of the supplier's key personnel, including email, phone number, and address.
- Supplier Certifications: Any certifications or accreditations held by the supplier, such as ISO certifications or industry-specific certifications.
- Supplier Performance History: Historical performance metrics and ratings for the supplier, including on-time delivery, quality metrics, and customer satisfaction.
- Supplier Financial Health: Financial information and indicators, such as revenue, profit margin, and credit ratings, to assess the financial stability and viability of the supplier.
- Supplier Risk Profile: Evaluation of the supplier's risk level, considering factors like compliance violations, legal issues, or supply chain disruptions.
- Supplier Compliance Data: Information related to the supplier's adherence to regulatory requirements, industry standards, and ethical practices.

In the transactional data system (e.g., SAP SRM), the metadata columns may include:

- Purchase Order (PO) Number: A unique identifier for each purchase order.

- Purchase Order Date: The date when the purchase order was created.
- Item Description: Description of the item or service being procured.
- Item Quantity: The quantity or volume of the item being procured.
- Unit Price: The price per unit of the item or service.
- Delivery Date: The expected delivery date for the item or service.
- Delivery Location: The location where the item or service should be delivered.
- Requester: The person or department who initiated the purchase request.
- Approver: The person or role responsible for approving the purchase order.
- Payment Terms: The agreed-upon terms and conditions for payment, such as net payment period or discounts.

In the Supplier Master data SAP system, the metadata columns may include:

- Supplier ID: Unique identifier for each supplier in the system.
- Supplier Name: The name or business entity of the supplier.
- Supplier Contact Information: Contact details of the supplier's key personnel, including email, phone number, and address.
- Supplier Type: Categorization of the supplier based on predefined types (e.g., manufacturer, distributor, service provider).
- Supplier Certification: Any certifications or accreditations held by the supplier, such as ISO

certifications or industry-specific certifications.

- Supplier Financial Information: Financial details of the supplier, including revenue, profit margin, and credit ratings.
- Supplier Performance History: Historical performance metrics and ratings for the supplier, including on-time delivery, quality metrics, and customer satisfaction.
- Supplier Risk Profile: Evaluation of the supplier's risk level, considering factors like compliance violations, legal issues, or supply chain disruptions.
- Supplier Compliance Data: Information related to the supplier's adherence to regulatory requirements, industry standards, and ethical practices.
- Supplier Relationship Manager: The designated person responsible for managing the relationship with the supplier.

These metadata columns provide valuable information for procurement processes, supplier evaluation, and decision-making within the organization. Please note that the availability of specific metadata columns may vary depending on the configuration and customization of the respective systems.

Now, once we have the visibility to all the three systems metadata, let us now analyze to see which data could be helpful for us to build a supplier scoring model.

As an example, we could consider the following fields in order to start building our model.

Metadata Column	Data Source
Supplier ID	*Supplier Master data SAP*
Supplier Name	*Supplier Master data SAP*
Supplier Location	*Supplier Master data SAP*
Supplier Contact Info	*Supplier Master data SAP*
Supplier Performance History: On-time Delivery Rate	*Transactional data system (e.g., SAP SRM)*
Supplier Performance History: Defect Rate	*Transactional data system (e.g., SAP SRM)*
Supplier Pricing Competitiveness	*Transactional data system (e.g., SAP SRM)*
Supplier Customer Satisfaction Ratings	*Transactional data system (e.g., SAP SRM)*
Supplier Performance in SAP Ariba Sourcing	*SAP Ariba sourcing data*

Let's consider sample data like the one shown in the table here.

Supplier ID	Supplier Name	Supplier Location	On-time Delivery Rate	Defect Rate	Pricing Competitiveness	Customer Satisfaction Ratings	Performance Metrics	Quality metrics	Supplier Performance in SAP Ariba Sourcing
S1	*Supplier 1*	*Location 1*	*90%*	*2%*	*High*	*4.5/5*	*4.5*	*9*	*Good*
S2	*Supplier 2*	*Location 2*	*95%*	*1.50%*	*Medium*	*4.2/5*	*3.25*	*8*	*Excellent*
S3	*Supplier 3*	*Location 3*	*88%*	*2.50%*	*Low*	*3.8/5*	*4.25*	*10*	*Fair*
S4	*Supplier 4*	*Location 4*	*92%*	*1%*	*High*	*4.7/5*	*3.75*	*7*	*Good*
S5	*Supplier 5*	*Location 5*	*91%*	*2.20%*	*Medium*	*4.3/5*	*4.0*	*9*	*Excellent*

Most of the time all the data shown in the table is directly not available. We might need to use some techniques in order to arrive to this data. For instance, let's say our organization is not capturing any kind of performance metrics or quality metrics for a supplier. An ideal approach to capture this could be gathering other data and computing/predicting these metrics.

Performance Metrics:

You can calculate performance metrics based on various factors such as on-time delivery, adherence to specifications, number of defects, customer satisfaction ratings, or any other relevant criteria. This may require collecting additional data or conducting surveys to gather feedback from stakeholders involved in supplier interactions.

Quality Metrics:

Quality metrics can be derived from various sources, including product or service inspections, audits, or compliance reports. You may need to assess factors such as product reliability, conformance to specifications, warranty claims, or any other relevant quality indicators from the supplier.

Clustering your data: Choose an appropriate clustering algorithm for your analysis. Popular unsupervised clustering algorithms include K-means, hierarchical clustering, and DBSCAN. We would need to consider factors such as the nature of data, the number of clusters you expect based on the domain expertise, and the interpretability of the results. Apply the selected clustering algorithm to your prepared data. The algorithm will group similar suppliers together based on their feature similarities. Each supplier will be assigned to a specific cluster.

Cluster Insights: Analyze the clusters obtained from the clustering algorithm. Explore the characteristics and patterns within each cluster to derive meaningful insights. You can use techniques like data visualization, descriptive statistics, and feature importance analysis to understand the unique traits and behavior of suppliers within each cluster.

Scoring the Suppliers: Based on the insights gained from the cluster analysis, define scoring criteria or rules that align with your organization's objectives and requirements.

Assign scores to each supplier based on their cluster membership and the corresponding insights. This can be done by defining thresholds or ranges for each relevant feature and mapping them to scores.

Outcome: The outcome is an AI-powered supplier scoring system that assigns scores to suppliers based on their historical data.

Impact on the organization: The AI-powered supplier scoring system improves the sourcing process by providing an objective and data-driven approach to evaluate and rank suppliers. It enhances decision-making, enables efficient supplier selection, and ultimately leads to improved supplier performance, reduced supply chain disruptions, and enhanced operational efficiency for the organization.

Predictive Demand Forecasting

Problem:

Demand forecasting can be done using various types of data, including transactional data (purchase order (PO) data), supplier master data, sourcing metadata from Ariba systems and contracts metadata from Ariba systems. Each of these data sources provides valuable insights that can contribute to accurate demand forecasting. Let us take a deep dive to see what each of these data sources contain and then analyze how each of them can be utilized. We may not be able to cover all the data features in each of the database systems over here. However, the idea here is to give you an overall feel of the data that could be available and how to make optimized use of it for creating a demand forecasting model.

Data used:

Let's consider a sample of the metadata you can extract from each source. The table below shows few of the important features that you can extract from each of the databases available.

Database System	Metadata	Description
Transactional Data (SAP SRM)	Order Date	The date when the purchase order was created
	Product/Item	The specific product or item being ordered
	Quantity	The quantity of the product ordered
	Price	The price per unit of the ordered product
	Supplier	The supplier from whom the product is ordered
Supplier Master Data	Supplier Name	The name of the supplier
	Supplier ID	A unique identifier for each supplier
	Supplier Location	The geographical location of the supplier
Contracts Metadata (SAP Ariba)	Contract ID	A unique identifier for each contract
	Contract Start Date	The date when the contract becomes effective
	Contract End Date	The date when the contract expires
	Contract Terms	Any specific terms or conditions mentioned in contract
Sourcing Metadata (SAP Ariba)	Sourcing Event ID	A unique identifier for each sourcing event
	Event Type	The type of sourcing event, such as RFP or RFQ
	Event Date	The date when the sourcing event took place
	Event Outcome	The result or outcome of the sourcing event

By combining and analyzing PO data, supplier data, and sourcing data, we can develop comprehensive demand forecasting models. So, now let us choose the data that we can combine in order to develop a demand forecasting model.

Data Source	Features
Transactional PO Data	Order Date, Product/Item, Quantity, Price
Supplier Master Data	Supplier Name, Supplier ID, Supplier Location
Contract Metadata from Ariba	Contract ID, Contract Start Date, Contract End Date, Contract Terms
Sourcing Metadata from Ariba	Sourcing Event ID, Event Type, Event Date, Event Outcome

Let us take an example to understand this better. The tables below show sample data for each of the data sources.

Transactional data:

Order Date	Product/Item	Quantity	Price	Supplier
1/1/2022	Item A	100	10.5	Supplier 1
1/2/2022	Item B	50	20	Supplier 2
1/3/2022	Item C	200	5	Supplier 1

Supplier Master Data:

Supplier Name	Supplier ID	Supplier Location
Supplier 1	1001	Location A
Supplier 2	1002	Location B

Contract Metadata from SAP Ariba:

Contract ID	Contract Start Date	Contract End Date	Contract Terms
C1001	1/1/2022	1/1/2023	Payment terms: 30 days
C1002	2/1/2022	2/1/2023	Minimum order quantity: 100 units

Sourcing metadata from Ariba:

Sourcing Event ID	Event Type	Event Date	Event Outcome
SE1001	RFP	3/1/2022	Supplier 1 selected
SE1002	RFQ	4/1/2022	Supplier 2 selected

Now, let us combine and see how a combined table that includes the primary keys and features from the Transactional PO Data, Supplier Master Data, Contract Metadata from Ariba, and Sourcing Metadata from Ariba looks like:

Order ID	Order Date	Product/Item	Quantity	Price	Supplier	Supplier ID	Supplier Location	Contract ID	Contract Start Date	Contract End Date	Contract Terms	Sourcing Event ID	Event Type	Event Date	Event Outcome
O1001	1/1/2022	Item A	100	10.5	Supplier 1	1001	Location A	C1001	1/1/2022	1/1/2023	Payment terms: 30 days	SE1001	RFP	3/1/2022	Supplier 1 selected
O1002	1/2/2022	Item B	50	20	Supplier 2	1002	Location B	C1002	2/1/2022	2/1/2023	Minimum order quantity: 100 units	SE1002	RFQ	4/1/2022	Supplier 2 selected
O1003	1/3/2022	Item C	200	5	Supplier 1	1001	Location A	C1002	2/1/2022	2/1/2023	Minimum order quantity: 100 units	SE1001	RFP	3/1/2022	Supplier 1 selected

In this table, the primary keys are:

- Order ID for Transactional PO Data
- Supplier ID for Supplier Master Data
- Contract ID for Contract Metadata from Ariba
- Sourcing Event ID for Sourcing Metadata from Ariba

This combined table allows you to have a comprehensive view of the relevant data from multiple sources, which can be used to build a demand forecasting model.

AI Model for demand forecasting:

Various forecasting algorithms can be used to build a demand forecasting model.

- Time Series Forecasting – Based on the order date for particular items, a time series model could be built to forecast the demand. An appropriate time series model for forecasting like ARIMA (AutoRegressive Integrated Moving Average), SARIMA (Seasonal ARIMA), or Prophet could be chosen based on the data patterns. The trained time series model would make predictions on new data points or future time periods. This will provide you with the forecasted demand.

- Regression Analysis - where machine learning algorithms like Random Forest, Gradient Boosting, or Neural Networks can be applied to forecast demand. These algorithms can handle complex relationships and nonlinear patterns in the data.

In the context of building a demand forecasting regression model using the provided sample data, the dependent feature, or the target variable, would typically be the "Quantity" column. The goal of the regression model would be to predict the quantity of a specific product based on the independent features (predictor variables) such as "Product/Item," "Supplier," "Order Date," "Price," and others.

The regression model would aim to establish a relationship between the dependent variable (Quantity) and the independent variables to predict the quantity of products for future orders. The model would analyze the historical data to identify patterns, trends, and correlations between the predictors and the target variable, allowing it to make predictions for new instances based on the learned relationship.

Outcome:

Building a demand forecasting model can have several outcomes and impacts on an organization:

- Improved Inventory Management: Accurate demand forecasting helps organizations optimize their inventory levels. By forecasting future demand, organizations can ensure they have the right amount of stock available, avoiding stockouts or excess inventory.

- Cost Savings: Effective demand forecasting enables organizations to optimize their procurement and production processes. With accurate forecasts, they can align their purchasing, production, and distribution activities, reducing costs associated with overstocking or understocking.

- Enhanced Customer Service: By accurately forecasting demand, organizations can meet customer expectations more effectively. They can ensure product availability, minimize backorders, and improve order fulfillment, resulting in increased customer satisfaction.

- Efficient Resource Allocation: Demand forecasting helps organizations allocate their resources efficiently. They can allocate production capacity, labor, and other resources based on anticipated demand, avoiding inefficiencies and improving overall operational performance.

- Strategic Decision-Making: With reliable demand forecasts, organizations can make informed strategic decisions related to product development, market expansion, and resource planning. This leads to better long-term planning and competitive advantage.

- Supply Chain Optimization: Demand forecasting facilitates supply chain optimization by enabling better coordination and collaboration with suppliers, distributors, and other partners. This helps in reducing lead times, improving delivery performance, and minimizing supply chain disruptions.

AI - Driven Contract Management

AI-driven contract management is a transformative application of artificial intelligence in the field of procurement. Contracts are essential components of business operations, governing relationships with suppliers, customers, and partners. However, we are all aware that contract management can be a complex and time-consuming process, involving tasks such as drafting, reviewing, and monitoring contracts for compliance.

With the power of AI, contract management becomes more efficient, accurate, and streamlined. AI algorithms can analyze and extract relevant information from contracts, such as terms, obligations, and deadlines, with remarkable speed and accuracy. Natural Language Processing (NLP) techniques enable computers to understand and interpret complex legal language, ensuring comprehensive contract analysis. Machine Learning algorithms can be trained on large volumes of contract data to identify patterns, risks, and opportunities, aiding in contract drafting, negotiation, and risk assessment.

The impact of AI-driven contract management is significant. It saves time and reduces manual effort, allowing procurement professionals to focus on more strategic tasks. AI can automatically flag potential risks, inconsistencies, or non-compliant clauses in contracts, enabling proactive risk management. It also improves contract visibility, making it easier to track and manage contract lifecycles, renewals, and obligations.

Here is a list of AI techniques that could be used to manage contracts effectively

- Natural Language Processing (NLP): NLP algorithms can be applied to extract key information from the contract, such as the contract title, effective date, supplier, buyer, term, scope, payment terms, and termination clause. This allows for automated and accurate contract analysis. Algorithms like BERT (Bidirectional Encoder Representations from

Transformers) or CRF (Conditional Random Fields), enable computers to understand and interpret complex legal language, ensuring comprehensive contract analysis.

- Named Entity Recognition (NER): NER models can identify and classify entities within the contract, such as company names, product names, dates, and payment terms. This helps in organizing and understanding the contract content more effectively. Here also any prebuilt language models like BERT can be used to transfer learn and then used on the organization data.

- Sentiment Analysis: Sentiment analysis models can be employed to assess the overall sentiment expressed in the contract. This can help identify any potentially contentious or unfavorable terms that may require attention during negotiation or review.

- Machine Learning for Risk Assessment: Machine learning algorithms can be trained on historical contract data to identify patterns and risks. By analyzing past contracts and their outcomes, the model can assess the risk associated with specific clauses or terms in the new contract, enabling better risk management and decision-making. Machine Learning algorithms, such as Random Forest or Support Vector Machines (SVM), can be trained on large volumes of contract data to identify patterns, risks, and opportunities, aiding in contract drafting, negotiation, and risk assessment.

A combination of one or more of the above techniques will lead to a well-defined problem that can be solved. Let's us take an example and try to understand this.

Contract Title: Supply Agreement
Effective Date: 1st January 2023
Supplier: XYZ Company
Buyer: ABC Corporation
Term: 3 years
Scope: Supplier agrees to provide ABC Corporation with 10,000 units of Product X per month at a price of $10 per unit.
Payment Terms: Net 30 days from the date of invoice.
Termination: Either party may terminate the agreement with 30 days' written notice.

For example, in a supply agreement contract, NLP algorithms can extract entities like contract title, effective date, supplier, buyer, term, scope, payment terms, and termination clause using Named Entity Recognition (NER) models like SpaCy or Stanford NER. Sentiment analysis models, such as VADER (Valence Aware Dictionary and sEntiment Reasoner), can be applied to assess the overall sentiment expressed in the contract. Machine Learning algorithms, like Logistic Regression or Decision Trees, trained on historical contract data can identify risks associated with specific clauses or terms, providing better risk assessment for contract management.

Virtual Assistants and Chatbots for Procurement

Virtual Assistants and Chatbots are transforming the way procurement activities are conducted by providing intelligent and interactive support. These AI-powered systems can understand natural language queries and assist users in various procurement tasks. They offer real-time assistance, automate routine inquiries, provide relevant information, and streamline the procurement process. Virtual Assistants and Chatbots utilize Natural Language

Processing (NLP) techniques, Machine Learning algorithms, and Knowledge Graphs to deliver personalized and context-aware responses.

A Virtual Assistant can help users find information about suppliers, track order status, provide pricing details, or guide them through procurement policies and procedures. It can leverage NLP algorithms like Intent Recognition and Named Entity Recognition to understand user queries and extract key information. Machine Learning algorithms, such as Deep Learning-based models or Reinforcement Learning, can enable Virtual Assistants to learn from user interactions and improve their responses over time.

Chatbots, on the other hand, can be integrated into messaging platforms or websites to provide instant support and facilitate procurement-related conversations. They can handle frequently asked questions, assist with order placement, offer recommendations, or provide updates on inventory availability. Chatbots utilize similar AI techniques, including NLP and Machine Learning, to understand and generate human-like responses.

The implementation of Virtual Assistants and Chatbots in procurement brings numerous benefits, including 24/7 availability, faster response times, improved user experience, and reduced operational costs. They empower procurement professionals by providing them with instant access to information and freeing up their time to focus on more strategic activities.

CHAPTER XVIII

Future Trends and Emerging Technologies in AI for Procurement

As I write this book, I am witnessing the rapid evolution of AI at an unprecedented pace. With new advancements and breakthroughs emerging almost every week, it is clear that technology, particularly in the field of AI, is progressing faster than ever before. The introduction of ChatGPT last year was just the beginning, and since then, the momentum has only accelerated. It seems as though AI is following its own version of Moore's Law, doubling in sophistication and capabilities in shorter and shorter time frames. It's like the genie is out of the bottle, and its power and potential are unstoppable.

I have observed this remarkable evolution firsthand, and it has inspired me to explore the future of procurement in the midst of this buzzing AI landscape. One of the most significant trends is the rise of generative AI, particularly large language models that have the capacity to revolutionize various sectors. By the time this book is published, these models may have already made their mark across industries. In this chapter, I delve into the possibilities of leveraging generative AI in procurement and the complexities that come with it. We will explore how this technology can be harnessed to drive efficiency and innovation in procurement processes.

Another area of exploration is blockchain technology. While it has been around for a few years, its widespread adoption has yet to be realized. However, it is worth examining if blockchain has the potential to enhance the efficiency and security of procurement operations. Together, we will dive into the concept of blockchain and its potential impact on procurement, exploring whether it can revolutionize the industry and drive greater transparency, traceability, and trust in supply chains.

In this chapter, we embark on a journey to explore the future possibilities of AI in procurement, considering the advancements in generative AI and the untapped potential of blockchain technology. By staying informed about these emerging trends, we can better navigate the evolving landscape of technology and leverage its transformative power to shape the future of procurement.

LLM's for Procurement

LLMs, which stands for Large Language Models, have been in existence for some time, albeit with limited capabilities. However, today we have LLMs such as GPT-3 and GPT-4 that surpass earlier models like BERT in terms of their capabilities. With these advanced LLMs, we can accomplish all the tasks previously discussed with NLP, but with even greater accuracy and precision. These new models have the potential to revolutionize natural language processing and enhance our ability to understand, interpret, and generate human-like text. By leveraging the power of these state-of-the-art LLMs, we can unlock new possibilities and achieve remarkable results in various applications, including procurement.

So, now what is so new about using LLM's in procurement?

The use of Large Language Models (LLMs) in procurement brings several new and exciting possibilities.

With the advancements in LLM technology, procurement professionals can harness the power of these models to automate and optimize various tasks. LLMs can be used for natural language understanding and generation, enabling more accurate and efficient communication with suppliers, stakeholders, and other procurement-related entities. By leveraging LLMs in procurement, organizations can benefit from enhanced supplier management, contract analysis, and demand forecasting. LLMs can help analyze and extract relevant information from contracts, enabling faster contract reviews and reducing the risk of errors. They can also assist in supplier selection and evaluation by analyzing vast amounts of supplier data, including performance metrics and customer feedback.

Furthermore, LLMs can be utilized to develop intelligent virtual assistants and chatbots for procurement, enabling self-service capabilities, faster response times, and improved user experiences. These virtual assistants can handle routine procurement inquiries, provide real-time information, and guide users through various procurement processes.

Generative AI

Generative AI is an emerging technology that holds great potential for transforming the field of procurement. Generative AI refers to AI models and algorithms that have the ability to generate new and original content, such as text, images, or even entire scenarios, based on patterns and examples learned from existing data. In the context of procurement, generative AI can be applied to various areas to improve efficiency, creativity, and decision-making.

One key application of generative AI in procurement is the generation of automated reports, summaries, and insights based on large volumes of data. By training AI models on historical procurement data, the generative AI system can analyze patterns, identify trends, and generate valuable insights that can aid in strategic decision-making and supplier management.

Generative AI can also be used for automating the creation of procurement documents and contracts. The system can learn from existing templates and contracts to generate new documents tailored to specific procurement scenarios, saving time and reducing the risk of errors. Additionally, generative AI can assist in the creation of realistic scenarios and simulations for procurement professionals to explore various what-if scenarios and evaluate the potential outcomes.

However, it is important to approach generative AI in procurement with caution and ensure ethical considerations are taken into account. As the technology becomes more sophisticated, there may be challenges related to bias, accountability, and transparency. It is essential to establish robust governance frameworks and ethical guidelines to mitigate these risks and ensure the responsible use of generative AI in procurement.

Blockchain and Smart Contracts in Procurement

Blockchain technology and smart contracts have gained significant attention in recent years, offering exciting possibilities for enhancing transparency, security, and efficiency in procurement processes. Blockchain is a decentralized and distributed ledger that records transactions across multiple nodes, ensuring transparency and immutability. Smart contracts, on the other hand, are self-executing contracts with the terms and conditions directly written into the code.

In the context of procurement, blockchain can provide a transparent and tamper-proof record of transactions, enabling increased trust and accountability between buyers and suppliers. By leveraging blockchain, organizations can track and verify the entire procurement lifecycle, including supplier selection, contract execution, and payment processes. This can help eliminate fraud, reduce disputes, and enhance the overall integrity of procurement operations.

Smart contracts further enhance the benefits of blockchain in procurement. These digital contracts are automatically executed when predefined conditions are met, eliminating the need for intermediaries and reducing administrative overhead. Smart contracts can facilitate the automation of key procurement processes, such as purchase orders, delivery verification, and payment settlements, streamlining operations and improving efficiency.

Moreover, blockchain technology can enable greater supply chain visibility and traceability. By recording transactions on a blockchain, organizations can track the movement of goods and verify their authenticity, ensuring compliance with regulatory requirements and addressing issues related to counterfeiting or unauthorized substitutions.

While blockchain and smart contracts offer immense potential, there are challenges to consider, such as scalability, interoperability, and data privacy. Implementing blockchain in procurement requires careful planning, collaboration, and investment in the right infrastructure and partnerships. Additionally, organizations must ensure compliance with relevant regulations and standards, as well as address concerns related to data privacy and security.

CHAPTER XIX

Ethical Considerations and Responsible AI in Procurement

Ethical AI is not just a choice, but a responsibility. As we navigate the uncharted territories of artificial intelligence, it is imperative that we uphold ethical principles to ensure that AI serves as a force for good, empowering humanity while safeguarding our values and preserving the dignity of every individual.

Ethical considerations and responsible AI practices are equally crucial in the context of procurement. As AI technologies continue to advance and become more integrated into procurement processes, it is essential to address potential ethical challenges and ensure that AI is used responsibly for the greater good. So, what is ethical AI in procurement?

In this chapter, let us try and understand the ethical dimensions of AI in procurement, examining key considerations that need to be taken into account. Data Privacy, Fairness and bias, Transparency and explain ability, accountability is few of the important dimensions that one needs to take care while building AI model to drive business.

Data Privacy

Data privacy is an essential consideration in the procurement domain, where handling sensitive information such as supplier details, contract terms, and financial transactions is commonplace. Safeguarding the privacy and confidentiality of this data becomes paramount when utilizing AI technologies. For instance, organizations can employ techniques like data anonymization or tokenization to protect personally identifiable information (PII) and ensure that sensitive data remains secure. By replacing identifiable information with unique identifiers or tokens, the privacy of individuals and organizations involved can be preserved while still enabling effective analysis and utilization of the data.

In a procurement scenario, when analyzing supplier performance, AI algorithms can process and evaluate historical data without directly exposing sensitive supplier information such as company names, addresses, or financial details. Instead, these details can be anonymized or tokenized, allowing the organization to derive meaningful insights and make informed decisions while respecting data privacy regulations and maintaining confidentiality.

Fairness and bias

Fairness and the mitigation of biases are essential considerations in AI-driven procurement to ensure equitable outcomes and avoid discrimination based on sensitive attributes. Algorithms and models can inadvertently perpetuate biases present in historical data, leading to unfair treatment or discriminatory practices. It is crucial to address these biases and strive for fairness in decision-making processes.

In supplier selection, an AI-driven system might use historical data to assess supplier performance and make recommendations. However, if the historical data exhibits bias towards certain suppliers based on factors like race or gender, the AI system could inadvertently perpetuate those biases and reinforce inequitable practices. To mitigate this, organizations can implement fairness-aware algorithms that identify and correct biases, ensuring that supplier evaluation is based on relevant and unbiased criteria. By incorporating fairness considerations into the design and training of AI models, organizations can enhance the fairness and inclusivity of their procurement processes.

Moreover, transparency and interpretability of AI systems are crucial in identifying and addressing biases. Organizations should strive to understand how AI models make decisions and which features or factors influence those decisions. This allows for the identification of potential biases and the necessary steps to mitigate them. By continuously monitoring and auditing AI systems, organizations can ensure that fairness is upheld throughout the procurement lifecycle.

Transparency and Explainability

Transparency and explainability play crucial roles in addressing ethical considerations when deploying AI in procurement. Stakeholders, including procurement professionals and suppliers, need to have a clear understanding of how AI models and algorithms make decisions. This understanding foster trust, promotes accountability, and enables stakeholders to identify and address any potential issues or biases.

For example, let's consider a scenario where an AI system is used to evaluate and rank suppliers based on various criteria, such as quality, cost, and delivery performance. The system produces a ranked list of suppliers, but stakeholders might question why a particular supplier received a certain ranking or why certain criteria were given more weight than others. In such cases, transparency and explainability become crucial in providing insights into the decision-making process.

By employing techniques like interpretability and explainable AI, organizations can shed light on the inner workings of AI models. This can involve visualizations, feature importance analysis, or providing explanations for individual decisions. For instance, an explainable AI system might reveal that a supplier received a lower ranking due to a history of late deliveries or inconsistent quality. This transparency allows stakeholders to comprehend the reasoning behind the AI system's decisions and enables them to engage in meaningful discussions, ask relevant questions, and provide feedback.

Accountability

Accountability is a fundamental consideration in the deployment of AI systems in procurement. As these systems become increasingly autonomous, it is crucial to establish clear lines of responsibility and ensure that decision-making processes can be traced back to accountable individuals or entities. By defining the roles and responsibilities of stakeholders involved in AI-enabled procurement processes, organizations can ensure that accountability is upheld throughout the entire procurement lifecycle.

Let's say an AI system is responsible for automatically approving purchase orders based on predefined rules and thresholds. In this scenario, accountability lies not only with the AI system itself but also with the individuals who design, develop, and maintain the system. Procurement professionals and AI specialists have the responsibility to establish the rules and criteria that guide the AI system's decision-making process. They must also monitor the system's performance, address any issues or biases that may arise, and continuously refine the system to align with changing business needs.

Additionally, accountability extends to the individuals who interact with the AI system. Users who rely on AI-generated recommendations or decisions should understand the limitations and assumptions of the system and exercise their judgment when necessary. They should also provide feedback and report any concerns or discrepancies they observe in the system's outputs.

To ensure accountability, organizations can implement mechanisms such as documentation and audit trails. These mechanisms allow for the tracking and recording of AI system activities, including the data used, the algorithms employed, and the decisions made. By maintaining a transparent record of the AI system's operations, organizations can conduct thorough reviews, address any issues that may arise, and attribute responsibilities when needed.

AI and Workforce Transformation in Procurement

The impact of AI on the workforce is a significant ethical consideration. As AI technologies automate certain tasks and processes, there is a concern about potential job displacement and the need for reskilling or upskilling the workforce to adapt to the changing landscape. It is crucial to approach this transition in a manner that fosters a supportive and inclusive environment for employees.

To address the ethical considerations of job displacement, the organization can take proactive steps to support its workforce. This may include offering training programs and resources to help employees acquire new skills that align with the evolving needs of the procurement function. By investing in upskilling initiatives, employees can acquire competencies in areas where AI may not yet excel, such as strategic decision-making, negotiation, and relationship management.

Additionally, organizations should foster a culture of continuous learning and create opportunities for employees to contribute to the development and improvement of AI systems. By involving employees in the AI implementation process and encouraging their feedback and insights, organizations can ensure that the technology is seen as a tool to augment their capabilities rather than replace them.

Organizations can also promote transparency and open communication about the integration of AI in procurement. This includes clearly communicating the objectives of implementing AI technologies, addressing concerns related to job displacement, and actively involving employees in the decision-making process. By fostering an inclusive environment, employees can feel empowered to adapt, collaborate, and explore new roles and responsibilities that arise from the integration of AI.

CHAPTER XX

Takeaways - Part 3

Before I wrap up the last part of this book, let me list down the key takeaways what we discussed in the previous 5 chapters.

- Definition of Advanced Analytics:

Advanced analytics refers to the use of advanced statistical, mathematical, and computational techniques to analyze large and complex data sets. It goes beyond traditional analytics methods and aims to uncover hidden patterns, correlations, and insights that can drive better decision-making.

- Techniques in Advanced Analytics:

Advanced analytics encompasses a wide range of techniques, including machine learning, data mining, predictive modeling, natural language processing (NLP), and artificial intelligence (AI). These methodologies allow businesses to make data-driven predictions and optimize their operations.

- Data and Data Quality:

The success of advanced analytics heavily depends on the quality and reliability of data. Organizations must ensure they have access to accurate and relevant data to derive meaningful insights. Data cleaning and preprocessing are essential steps before applying advanced analytics techniques.

- Machine Learning:

Machine learning is a subset of advanced analytics that focuses on building algorithms and models that enable computers to learn from data without explicit programming. It has applications in image recognition, natural language processing, recommendation systems, and more.

- Predictive Analytics:

Predictive analytics involves using historical data and machine learning models to make predictions about future events or outcomes. It helps businesses anticipate customer behavior, demand patterns, and potential risks.

- Prescriptive Analytics:

Prescriptive analytics takes predictive analysis a step further by suggesting optimal actions to achieve specific outcomes. It combines historical data, predictions, and business rules to recommend the best course of action.

- Challenges and Considerations:

While advanced analytics can be powerful, it comes with challenges. Organizations must address data privacy and security concerns, interpretability of models, and the need for skilled data scientists and analysts to implement and interpret results.

- Ethical Implications:

Advanced analytics raises ethical considerations regarding data privacy, bias in algorithms, and the potential impact on individuals and society. Organizations must adopt responsible practices to ensure fair and ethical use of data.

- Continuous Learning and Improvement:

Advanced analytics is a dynamic field with constant advancements. Organizations should foster a culture of continuous learning and improvement to stay updated with the latest technologies and methodologies.

Before You Leave

Thanks for reading the book this far. I hope you hace enjoyed the way I collated my thoughts on digital transformation based on my research and experience. We have together walked through the journey of exploring digitalization of the procurement process, uncovering the potential it holds to revolutionize the way organizations manage and improve operational efficiency. We discussed in depth the key three areas: Data handling, Analytics Adventure, and AI innovation. Now, as we reach the end of this book, let me summarize the valuable insights gained and address any lingering issues, ensuring a comprehensive and satisfying conclusion to our exploration.

Hopefully, you are now convinced that data handling forms the foundation of digital procurement transformation. We have understood the significance of accurate and accessible data, emphasizing the need for robust systems to collect, store, and analyze information effectively. Implementing modern data management practices and leveraging advanced technologies, organizations can streamline their procurement processes, reduce errors, and gain valuable insights. The concept of a data lake remains the core, in order to get our basic data right and easy access. We are also now in a position to assess the challenges that would come along the way while integrating data. Not just knowing them, but we also now know how to tackle these challenges. Data management systems design is a most critical starting point in this journey, and by now we are well equipped as to how we tackle this.

Once data problems are solved, we saw how the Analytics adventure unraveled the power of data analysis in procurement. We witnessed how analytics could help us to build our meaningful dashboards to extract patterns, trends, and actionable intelligence from vast amounts of data. Now with the knowledge of these capabilities, you could help your organizations make informed decisions through descriptive and diagnostic analytics to optimize supplier relationships and identify cost-saving opportunities. Analytics serves as a compass, guiding procurement professionals towards data-driven excellence.

Taking a deep dive into analytics, keep moving ahead to predictive and prescriptive analytics. Our exploration culminated in the realm of AI innovation. You are now aware of the transformative potential of artificial intelligence in procurement, from intelligent automation to predictive machine learning. The knowledge of AI-driven technologies that empower organizations to automate routine tasks, enhance decision-making, mitigate risks, and drive efficiency across the procurement lifecycle makes you think beyond the legacy procurement processes. You would now agree that by embracing these innovations, procurement professionals can unlock new levels of productivity and strategic value. Well, at this point when Generative AI is around, it would be imperative to think about the immense potential this could add on to the journey of procurement digitalization. Large language models that are around are no doubt game-changers in the way we could leverage AI for the procurement process. Do you agree? If not, just think about the thousands of contracts/SOWs/MSAs with unstructured data lying in front of you. How would you make machines start to talk to these documents? And the answer is Gen AI!

As I conclude this book, I want to ensure that everything is wrapped up in a bow, leaving no loose ends. It is essential to recognize that the digitalization of procurement is not a one-size-fits-all solution. Each organization is unique, with varying goals, resources, and challenges. So, what we read and understood till this point is a generalized framework. However, the principles discussed throughout this book provide a solid foundation for embarking on your digital procurement journey. Can I now say that it has started to provoke your thought process?

Now, the call to action is to embrace the digital transformation of procurement within your organization. Start by assessing your current processes, identifying pain points. Well, it's not always easy for people to describe their pain points. In a routine day-to-day work setup, many of them do not realize what their pain points could be. Envisioning the desired state of your digital procurement ecosystem is the ideal way to start. Comparing and finding the gap between what people are doing today vs. what people need to do in the future is what we need to understand. This at least sets the plot, and we could start to think of the actions that are to be done. Asking repeated questions on the problem statement that is defined is a good way to identify the root cause. It's not always an analytical solution; sometimes, the problems could be something else. Maybe fixing a behavioral issue could be the solution.

Engage key stakeholders, including procurement teams, IT departments, and senior management, to foster a shared vision of the future and secure the necessary support and resources. Communication among cross-platform specialists is the key to achieving the true potential. The right team involvement is very crucial. We can definitely not expect procurement professionals to design the architecture of the IT system, similarly, a Software Solutions Architect cannot ever imagine a procurement problem that needs to be solved. We would need specialists from various backgrounds - especially from the process team to help in defining the problem statements clearly, data management, analytics engineers & data scientists to enable you to design the paradigm of your digital journey, IT solution architects to deliver the solution as a whole to the organization. A niche requirement would be people who would understand both the process and the technology - though it is very difficult to find.

To further support your efforts, I would encourage you to explore additional resources available. Find case studies, whitepapers, and webinars on digital procurement best practices. Join industry forums and engage with like-minded professionals to exchange insights and lessons learned. Well, as you know - continuous learning and knowledge sharing are paramount to stay at the forefront of this rapidly evolving field.

In conclusion, the digital transformation of procurement holds immense promise for organizations seeking to drive sustainable competitive advantage. By mastering data handling, embarking on an analytics adventure, and embracing AI innovation, you are poised to revolutionize your procurement processes and deliver substantial value to your organization. So, take the leap, embrace the digital revolution, and unlock the full potential of procurement in the digital age.

Thank you for joining me on this enlightening journey. May your digital procurement endeavors be fruitful and transformative!

Would love to hear your suggestions and feedback on this.

Get in touch with me on

LinkenIn

https://www.linkedin.com/in/deepti-bandi-3ba17a1b/

or email me at

deeptibandi@gmail.com

www.ingramcontent.com/pod-product-compliance
Lightning Source LLC
La Vergne TN
LVHW050540160826
845677LV00011B/2104

* 9 7 9 8 8 9 0 6 7 2 0 6 3 *